COTTON TENANTS

JAMES AGEE

COTTON

THREE

WALKER EVANS

TENANTS

FAMILIES

Edited by John Summers   *Preface by Adam Haslett*

BROOKLYN · LONDON

COTTON TENANTS: THREE FAMILIES

Text © 2013 The James Agee Trust

Photographs by Walker Evans are reprinted from the the two-volume album *Photographs of Cotton Sharecropper Families*, held by the Library of Congress Prints and Photographs Division.

Cover photograph: Walker Evans, *Floyd Burroughs and Tingle Children, Hale County, Alabama*, 1936. Courtesy of the Library of Congress.

Design by Christopher King

Melville House Publishing   8 Blackstock Mews
145 Plymouth Street   and   Islington
Brooklyn, NY 11201   London N4 2BT

mhpbooks.com

First Melville House Printing: May 2013

ISBN: 978-1-61219-212-3

Printed in the United States of America
3 5 7 9 10 8 6 4 2

A catalog record for this title is available
from the Library of Congress.

"Despair so far invading every tissue has destroyed in these the hidden seats of the desire and of the intelligence."

W. H. Auden

CONTENTS

Editor's Note

James Agee never lacked for recognition as a poet, film critic, or screenwriter. So much more was expected of him, though. He couldn't shake the suspicion that his talent was wasted even before his health wound down. "Nothing much to report," he wrote in a May 11, 1955, letter. "I feel, in general, as if I were dying: a terrible slowing-down, in all ways, above all in relation to work." When he succumbed five days later, he was forty-five. It would be three more years before his novel *A Death in the Family* appeared and won its enduring acclaim. It had been a long time since anyone had mentioned his obscure book about tenant farmers in Alabama, *Let Us Now Praise Famous Men*.

"Cotton Tenants" marked Agee's first attempt to tell the story of that momentous trip. Commissioned in the summer of 1936, only to be shelved by *Fortune* magazine— Agee was a staff writer—the typescript wasted away in his Greenwich Village home for nearly twenty years, a piercing fragment lodged within a collection of unread manuscripts. But Agee's young daughter inherited both the home and the collection, and eventually (in 2003, to be specific) she cleared it out. Two years later, the James Agee Trust transferred the collection to the University of Tennessee Special Collections Library; there, all the papers were cataloged, and "Cotton Tenants" was discovered among the remains.

Although no date appeared on the typescript, there's no good reason to believe Agee wrote a later draft or that this isn't the one his editors declined to publish. As far as I know, no other versions of "Cotton Tenants" exist in any archive, public or private. Nor is it possible, then, to know with certainty the story behind the two appendices, "On Negroes" and "Landowners"—both placed here exactly as found on the typescript. This pair of notes suggest, however, "the gigantic weight of physical and spiritual brutality [the Negro] has borne and is bearing" was not far from his closest perceptions.

As soon as I became aware of the existence of the typescript (in 2010, to be specific), I did the only decent thing and asked the Agee Trust for permission to publish part of it in *The Baffler*. About one-third of "Cotton Tenants" first appeared in issue 19, which was released in March 2012. A partnership was then struck between *The Baffler* and Melville House to bring out the complete report, and the result is before you. It is published for the first time here—an act of love for the author.

Kelly Burdick, Hugh Davis, Melissa Flashman, Lindsey Gilbert, David Herwaldt, John T. Hill, Eliza LaJoie, Michael Lofaro, Paul Sprecher, Rob Vanderlan, and David Whitford all had a hand in bringing about this publication. The photos and captions in this volume were selected from Walker Evans's two-volume album, *Photographs of Cotton Sharecropper Families*, held by the Library of Congress Prints and Photographs Division.

—John Summers, *The Baffler*

A Poet's Brief

ADAM HASLETT

How to attend to suffering and injustice? There is so much of it. If we move through the world with our ears and eyes open, it is all around us. It seems intractable. We need filters to prevent ourselves from being swamped, classifications to remove our experience of the pain of others to a level of endurable abstraction. By the time we become adults—if we become adults—this adaptation has taken place without our much noticing it. There are friends and family, whose suffering is ineluctable. There are people in the immediate communities, physical and virtual, that we live in whose troubles we see and talk about. And then there is the pain of distant others, people who live in places we've never been, news of whose suffering arrives through the media, if it arrives at all. It comes as sheer blight, implicating us we know not how. This we either attempt to ignore or treat as an "issue," an altogether more tractable entity.

Yet some social visionaries and brokenhearted artists, of whom James Agee was one, fail richly to make this adaptation. Their work, in the manner of Jesus strained through Marx, insists that distinctions between the suffering of intimates and the suffering of strangers are an outrage. With strenuous empathy they report or represent the hardship of the poor and the disenfranchised. The result is a kind of morally indignant anthropology. An ethnography delivered from the pulpit. Which more or less describes *Cotton Tenants: Three Families*, James Agee's report on the working conditions of poor white farmers in the Deep South.

Fortune magazine commissioned the report in the summer of 1936, sending Agee and the photographer Walker Evans to Alabama, and then refused to publish it. No firm evidence has ever surfaced to suggest precisely why. One might ask, though, how any minion in Henry Luce's magazine empire, which included *Time* and *Life* as well as *Fortune*, could have expected such a thing to be published.

Agee, born in Knoxville in 1909, joined *Fortune* as a staff writer in 1932, straight out of Harvard, where he'd executed a parody of Luce's slick, soul-crushing conception of journalism in the *Harvard Lampoon*, while at the same time getting in his digs on "that high-falutin flub-drubbery which is Harvard." He arrived at his office on the fifty-second floor of the Chrysler Building with a reputation as a poet. (*Permit Me Voyage*, his first book, won the Yale Series of Younger Poets award in 1934.) Luce believed poets and writers could be taught to expand on the subject of business and invested *Fortune*'s pages with an almost cinematic juxtaposition of words and images. The managing editor Ralph Ingersoll assigned the young poet long, intricate stories on the cultural interests of the overlords amid the ongoing Depression.

Agee wrote of the blood sport of cockfighting ("a minor and surreptitious pleasure of the rich"), the boredom and decay of Roman aristocracy in Mussolini's Italy ("there are parties here and parties there but they are mostly neither here nor there"), Saratoga's summer horse racing gambol, the "U.S. Commercial Orchid," and so on. These stories leave no doubt that business journalism can be turned into a kind of literature, or that Agee was keenly talented at the sort of long-form writing that's become all but extinct in our own time. His 1933 story on the Tennessee Valley Authority, his first important assignment, earned him a personal commendation from Luce, who told him it was among the best *Fortune* writing ever printed.

In the summer of 1936, though, when *Fortune* asked

him to travel to Alabama to investigate the lives of cotton tenants for the magazine's Life and Circumstances department, he greeted the assignment with no small amount of apprehension. He convinced his editors to pair him with Walker Evans, a friend then at the Resettlement Administration, but doubted his own ability to see the story through. "Best break I ever had on *Fortune*," he wrote in a June 18 letter, two days before the pair left New York for Alabama, on their epic road trip into feudal capitalism, Southern-style. "Feel terrific responsibility toward story; considerable doubts of my ability to bring it off; considerable more of *Fortune*'s unwillingness to use it as it seems (in theory) to me."

Agee's frustration with Luce's brand of journalism wasn't new. "It varies with me from a sort of hard, masochistic liking without enthusiasm or trust, to direct nausea at the sight of this symbol $ and this % and this biggest and this some blank billion," he'd written to a friend the year before his breakthrough assignment to Alabama. "But in the long run I suspect the fault, dear *Fortune*, is in me: that I hate any job on earth, as a job and hindrance and semisuicide." A colleague once reported finding him dangling outside his office window.

Agee was already developing a sense of himself as a stranger and a spy at *Fortune*, a poet trapped in the tower of the Chrysler Building. This double alienation—this feeling of being at home neither in the office in New York nor, it turned out, on the harsh cotton fields of Alabama— infused the trip with a great emotional tension. "The trip was very hard, and certainly one of the best things I've ever had happen to me," he wrote in September, after spending two months with and among the families. "Writing what we found is a different matter. Impossible in any form and length *Fortune* can use; and I am now so stultified trying to do that, that I'm afraid I've lost the ability to make it right in my own way."

As Agee struggled to find a form that suited his vision—one of his drafts reached eighty pages—a new managing editor discontinued the magazine's Life and Circumstances series. In the end, the magazine held the 30,000-word report that Agee wound up submitting for a year, then killed it. Precisely why, nobody can say for sure—there are no telltale letters from his editor, no clear proof he refused to cooperate, nothing nearly so neat and tidy from either side. Politics, no doubt, played a part. Who knows how many subversive stories of the Great Depression were killed off, or never considered, by the reign of money's prerogatives in the respectable press. What we do know is that the many and subtle adaptations that made possible Agee's previous and subsequent writing for the magazine failed in this case, and failed momentously.*

The next summer, Agee rented a house in French-town, New Jersey, and summed up his discontent with a position that he never surrendered. "I am essentially an anarchist," he wrote. Introducing the book that he eventually produced, *Let Us Now Praise Famous Men*, he conveyed nothing but scorn for the cutting-edge radicals, artists, and reformers hovering around the subject of cotton tenantry, and singled out Luce-like journalism for special contempt. "The very blood and semen of journalism is a broad and successful form of lying," he wrote. "Remove that form of lying and you no longer have journalism." *Let Us Now Praise Famous Men* sold six hundred copies in its first year, a few thousand more in remainder, and went out of print. Not until 1960, five years after Agee's death, was it republished and recognized as a classic of American literature. And not until now, seventy-seven years after he wrote it, is the report he submitted available.

*The best and most detailed and balanced examination of this history is found in Robert Vanderlan's *Intellectuals Incorporated: Politics, Art, and Ideas Inside Henry Luce's Media Empire* (Philadelphia: University of Pennsylvania Press, 2010).

Cotton Tenants, published here for the first time, is a good deal more than source material for *Let Us Now Praise Famous Men*. At first blush, it is tempting to view what follows in this way because much of the physical description and some of the organizing principles of the report are carried through into the book. But the two works are very different. *Let Us Now Praise Famous Men* is a four-hundred-page sui generis prose symphony on the themes of poverty, rural life, and human existence. *Cotton Tenants* is a poet's brief for the prosecution of economic and social injustice. The former, as Agee himself tells us, is meant to be sung; the latter, preached.

And the message is unsettling: "A civilization which for any reason puts a human life at a disadvantage; or a civilization which can exist only by putting human life at a disadvantage; is worthy neither of the name nor of continuance." Those who are willing to benefit from the disadvantage of others are "human being[s] by definition only, having much more in common with the bedbug, the tapeworm, the cancer, and the scavengers of the deep sea." Agee's aim is to excite the reader's outrage by describing the particular disadvantages of tenant farmers in meticulous detail. He begins with their economic plight: they are trapped on their land in a credit system that makes it next to impossible to pay back the debts they keep racking up to their landlords for rent, manure, seed, and the money to feed and clothe themselves. With bad weather, a year's labor can leave them with more debt than they began with.

Agee anatomizes these arrangements through the prisms of food, shelter, clothing, work, leisure, education, and a typical Saturday trip to the nearest town. At the time he went to Alabama with Agee, Walker Evans was working for the Resettlement Administration, whose director, Roy Stryker, had described part of his agency's goal as "introducing America to Americans." And this is the documentary approach the report takes, introducing the subscribers of *Fortune* to the Burroughs, Tingle, and Fields families, as if to a country they didn't know existed.

Much of the detail of the families' daily lives is delivered in flat, declarative sentences. But a full page rarely goes by without at some point rising into a higher, poetic register. On a summer afternoon, a woman rests "beneath a flyswarmed floursack, and her children convolve in any chance stage between heat-enchanted silence and rampant cruelty against each other or the animals." The families go to Moundville on Saturday, "drawn in out of the slow and laborious depths of the country, along the withered vine of their red roadsteads and along the sedanswept blue slags of highway, on mule, on mule-drawn wagon and by foot hanging together, each family, like filings delicately aligned by a hidden magnet." Just as Evans's photographs did, Agee's words make the quotidian epic. The gently concussive rhythms and repetitions, the seemingly immemorial, even involuntary, motions (filings to a magnet), provide the musical underpinning to the explicit theme of people caught in a circle of work and debt over which they have little or no power.

But why, seventy-seven years later, should we spend time reading a piece of rejected journalism about a vanished world? The agricultural arrangements it describes are gone; the extreme material poverty and malnutrition it documents are no longer widespread conditions in the American South; and the patterns of social life it captures are a thing of the past.

One answer lies in the example it sets for the scope and tenor of journalistic inquiry. What follows is an unapologetic attack on a hidebound class system, an attack firmly grounded in the lived particulars of those near the bottom of the order. Yet it is not simply a piece of muckraking. There is no specific scandal or perfidy personified by an evil landlord. At the outset, Agee makes clear (partly to fit the series in *Fortune* for which the piece had been commissioned) that the families he's describing are not the worst cases, but representative ones; the worst cases, he says, would distract through voyeurism. Shock stuns the mind, and by that very action can often engender lassitude. We gaze in horror and then turn away in what becomes a kind of sentimental entertainment. The way out of this trap is to link the lives described with the system that creates their conditions. To give an analysis of politics that's firmly grounded in the actual results of politics. This involves more than "providing context," as the standard journalistic nostrum puts it. It requires combining political intelligence with writerly intelligence—that is, the apprehension of human character and creaturely habit.

Here is Agee:

> The essential structure of the South is, of course, economic: cold and inevitable as the laws of chemistry. But that is not how the machine is run. The machine is run on intuition, and the structures of intuition are delicate and subtle as they can be only in a society which is not merely one thing but two: a dizzy mixture of feudalism and of capitalism in its latter stages.

Yes, there is a system, and it can be outlined in the abstract, but to understand how and why it persists you have to understand the "structures of intuition," the daily modes of being, the fears and aspirations that allow it to continue, that permit dehumanization to be perceived as natural law. The small-time capitalism of the landlords maintains itself partly on the vestiges of feudal deference given by farmers stuck on their land. This uneasy relationship is managed by the shared intuition of white supremacy. The white farmers Agee profiles may be poor, but there are always black farmers who are poorer and more abjectly treated than they are. It's part of the structure of sentiments that helps to hold the economic hierarchy in place.

Cotton Tenants presses us to ask two questions: What, precisely, are the economic mechanisms that enforce our own class hierarchies? And what are the "structures of intuition" that serve as the social glue of the system? Providing the answers is the task of engaged journalism: to tell us the story of our own economic collapse and the pain it continues to cause. It is not difficult to see the outlines. Real wages for the working class have been declining for forty years. The increases in "efficiency" and "labor productivity" celebrated by economists have become a transfer mechanism from the poor and middle class to the owners of capital. Wage earners work longer for less; investors reap the rewards.

Global competition plays its part in this equation,

serving as a seemingly permanent brake on workers' ability to demand higher wages. It also points up the need for journalists to cover the forms of indentured servitude and the "dizzy mixture of feudalism and of capitalism in its latter stages" that are still very much alive, from Chinese factories to Indian sweatshops to labor camps in Abu Dhabi, and that are more directly related than ever to our own gaping divide in wealth and well-being.

You don't have to look hard to see how our own credit system, administered not by small-time landlords but by banks, credit-rating companies, and collection agencies, has established an impersonal, finance-capitalist variant of the debt trap Agee described seventy-seven years ago. In what some economists wryly call "privatized Keynesianism," the United States, by deregulating financial institutions over the last thirty years, puffed a credit bubble, creating consumer demand by encouraging high levels of personal indebtedness. States repealed usury laws capping credit card interest rates, and when these contributed to dramatically higher levels of personal bankruptcies, Congress stepped in to make it harder to escape credit card debt in bankruptcy courts. Workers pay the interest on their debt out of stagnant wages, transferring even more money from poor and working people to the wealthy. Working-class people who manage to enter college leave with punishing levels of debt (amazingly, aggregate student debt in the United States now surpasses aggregate credit card debt) and then face the worst job market in generations. It is harder to escape poverty and move up the class ladder in the United States than it is in most Western European countries, including Britain and France, whose class rigidities seem so much more apparent on the surface.

If this is the system, then what is the social glue that holds it together? Again, this requires the granular description of actual lives, but we could begin with mass identification with the rich and the famous. Ours has long been a lottery culture, in which we are—all of us—protorich. We are fed a constant diet of stories by the corporate media chronicling the extraordinary rise of everyday people into a life of ease and luxury. For a generation, the image of the superwealthy was of a lone software inventor who started his/her business in a garage, rather than the head of a trust in New York who bought and sold only money.

That, interestingly and hopefully, has begun to change. If the crash of 2008 and the protests that followed did anything for us, they made unavoidable some journalistic attention to class power—how wealth in the United States breeds advantage, which breeds more wealth and more advantage, not through labor or smarts but simply as a privilege of already being on top. This was always true, of course; it has just been hidden in plain sight for a very long time.

As long as people on the bottom and the shrinking middle of the income scale continue to imagine themselves as future members of the ruling elite, there is no possibility of class politics. Aspirational marketing fogs our brains and hides reality. But perhaps now more people previously loyal to the system are beginning to understand how rigged it is. Close and thorough description of people's actual circumstances in the manner of Agee's long-form report from Alabama, applied to our own time, would doubtless help burn off some of that fog, waking us from the fantasy that we can all earn or win lottery sums. Of such conscience-stricken journalism the aim isn't to depress anyone's ambition; it's to understand how the world functions. There will always be exceptions to the rules. But if we don't understand the rules, we can't change them. That goes for the cruelties of capitalism as well as the sentiments that grant it the appearance of common sense.

Introduction

JAMES AGEE

The cotton belt is sixteen hundred miles wide and three hundred miles deep. Sixty per cent of those whose lives depend directly on the cotton raised there, between eight and a half million men, women, and children, own no land and no home but are cotton tenants. This article is a detailed account of the lives of three families of them, chosen with all possible care to represent the whole. None of the three families written of here could alone show or even fairly suggest that whole. Together, they at least suggest it. They work neither for that worst type of landlord, the absentee (human being or corporation) and his manager and riding boss; nor for that "best" type, the paternalist. They work land whose yield approximates the national average. One runs a two-mule

PREVIOUS SPREAD: HOUSE, HALE COUNTY

farm. Two are of that nominally more fortunate class of tenant which works on third and fourth. One is a repository for much that is the worst that poverty in the rural South can do to a white human being; one is much cleaner and more "self-respecting" than the average (with no happier results); the third cradles and interweaves a number of differences between. In the effort to avoid the least appearance of the bias which has made a good deal of reporting on the subject suspect, we have concentrated upon the Burroughs, that one of the three families which presents the least flagrant picture.

No serious study of any aspect of cotton tenancy would be complete without mention at least of the landlord and of the Negro: one tenant in three is a Negro. But this is not their story. Any honest consideration of the Negro would crosslight and distort the issue with the problems not of a tenant but of a race: any fair discussion of landholders would involve us in economic and psychological problems which there is room only to indicate here.

Readers who find this account lacking in detail

of violence and of the more flagrant forms of blood-squeezing and of cheating will do ill to conclude either that they do not exist or that we have preferred to avoid mention of them; and will do well to bear a few facts in mind. That those forms of cheating, though generally enough distributed, are not necessarily unanimous. That violence, which quite certainly, anywhere in that country, is the reply to any gesture distinctly unsettling to the landowners, is not yet by any means representative of the country as a whole because the population as a whole is still kept tidily in line by its own ignorance and by the certain knowledge of what happens when you step out of line, in other words by fear. That tenants are quite properly not eager to communicate information which, published under their names and pictures, would entail unemployment and physical danger. And that if the life of the tenant is as bad as it has been painted—and it is worse—it will show its evil less keenly, essentially and comprehensively in the fate of the worst-treated than in that steady dripping of daily detail which effaces the lives even of the relatively "well" treated.

1. The Great Ball on which we live.

The world is our home. It is also the home of many, many other children, some of whom live in far-away lands. They are our world brothers and sisters.

2. Food, Shelter, and Clothing.

What must any part of the world have in order to be a good home for man? What does every person need in order to live in comfort? Let us imagine that we are far out in the fields. The air is bitter cold and the wind is blowing. Snow is falling, and by and by it will turn into sleet and rain. We are almost naked. We have had nothing to eat and are suffering from hunger as well as cold. Suddenly the Queen of the Fairies floats down from the clouds and offers us three wishes.

What shall we choose?

"I shall wish for food, because I am hungry," says Peter.

"I shall choose clothes to keep out the cold," says John.

"And I shall ask for a house to shelter me from the wind, the snow, and the rain," says little Nell with a shiver.

Now everyone needs food, clothing, and shelter. The lives of most men on the earth are spent in getting these things. In our travels we shall wish to learn what our world brothers and sisters eat and where their food comes from. We shall wish to see the houses they dwell in and how they are built. We shall wish also to know what clothing they use to protect themselves from the heat and cold.

These are the opening sentences from *Around the World With the Children*, a third grade geography textbook belonging to Lucile Burroughs, aged ten, daughter of a cotton tenant.

The world is our home. Human life, we must assume in the first place, is somewhat more important than anything else in human life, except, possibly, what happens to it. It deserves attention, and a seriousness of attention, commensurate with its importance. And since every possibility human life holds, or may be deprived of, of value, of wholeness, of richness, of joy, of dignity, depends all but entirely upon circumstances, the circumstances are proportionately worthy of the serious attention of anyone who dares to think of himself as a civilized human being. A civilization which for any reason puts a human life at a disadvantage; or a civilization which can exist only by putting human life at a disadvantage; is worthy neither of the name nor of continuance. And a human being whose life is nurtured in an advantage which has accrued from the disadvantage of other human beings, and who prefers that this should remain as it is, is a human being by definition only, having much more in common with the bedbug, the tapeworm, the cancer, and the scavengers of the deep sea.

Only if we hold such truths to be self-evident, and inescapable, and quite possibly more serious and

BURROUGHS' WORK SHOES

quite certainly more immediate than any others, may we in any honesty and appropriateness proceed to our story: which is a brief account of what happens to human life, and of what human life can in no essential way escape, under certain unfavorable circumstances.

The circumstances, that is to say, out of which and into which the cotton tenant is born; and under the steady raining of which he stands up the years into his distorted shape; and beneath the reach of which he declines into death. The fact that his circumstances are merely local specializations of the huge and the ancient, all but racial circumstance of poverty: of a life so continuously and entirely consumed into the effort merely and barely to sustain itself; so profoundly deprived and harmed and atrophied in the courses of that effort, that it can be called life at all only by biological courtesy: this fact should not confuse and indeed can only sharpen our discernment. We would be dishonest for instance to cheer ourselves with the thought that in ameliorating the status of the cotton tenant alone, any essential problem whatever would be solved: and we would be merely fools to comfort ourselves with the reflection that the South is a "backward" country.

Our story, however, is limited. We would tell you only of the living three families, chosen with all possible care fully and fairly to represent the million and a quarter families, the eight and a half to nine million human beings, who are the tenant farmers of the cotton belt.

The families are those of Floyd Burroughs, and of Bud Fields his father-in-law, and of Fields's half-brother-in-law Frank Tingle. They live on a lift of redland called Mills Hill, in Hale County, in west central Alabama. Fields and Tingle work for the brothers and partners J. Watson and J. Christopher Tidmore, who live in Moundville, a small town ten red clay and five highway miles north of them. Burroughs works for Fletcher Powers, who lives a couple of miles south of Moundville. We shall begin with an outline of those business arrangements between the tenant Floyd Burroughs and the landowner Fletcher Powers whereby Burroughs, and his wife, and their four children, live.

CHAPTER I

Business

Burroughs furnishes his labor, and the labor of his family.

Powers furnishes the plant, the supplies, and the money. That is to say, he furnishes the land, the house on it, the outbuildings, the water supply, the garden plot, the directions on what to plant where, when, and how, the tools, the seed, the mule, half the mule feed, rations money, half the fertilizer and, for the time being, Burroughs's half of the fertilizer.

Burroughs pays off his rent by turning over half the cotton, half the cottonseed, and half the corn he makes. (Some landlords take half of the peas and half of the sorghum, too.)

His own half of the corn, he keeps to bread his family and to feed the mule during the half of the year he has the mule.

Off his own half of the cottonseed, once his half

of the ginning fee is paid, he gets the money he lives on during the picking season.

All the money he gets from his half of the cotton is his own, after he has paid back the rations money that was advanced him at eight per cent interest, and any other debts, such as doctor bills, that may be outstanding.

The rest of the money is clear cash money, with which to buy the shoes and clothes that are by that time badly needed; with which to buy at least a few pretties for the young ones at Christmas time; and on which to live through the hardest months of the year.

Under this arrangement he is what is known as a halvers-hand, or as a sharecropper.

If Burroughs owned a mule and tools, like Bud Fields, or tools and two mules, like Frank Tingle, he would like them be working on third and fourth, or he would be called a tenant.*

Fields and Tingle work under much the same arrangement, but furnish their own seed, and two-thirds of the guano they use (on their cotton) and

*The proper generic word is *tenant*. Northern journalism has made *sharecropper* an inaccurate cover-all.

three-fourths of the soda they use (on their corn), and pay, as rent, only a third of their cotton and cotton-seed and a fourth of their corn.

Very few tenants keep books. Of those who do, still fewer are so foolish as to bring them up for comparison with the landlord's. It is not only that no landlord, nor influential citizen, nor any court of law, would give his accounting any credit against his landlord's. It is, more importantly, that any questioning of the landlord's word would create an extremely unfavorable impression. Such a tenant would not be the type of willing worker a landlord would care to keep on his place. Moreover, any other landlord the tenant tried moving to would feel the same about it; and so would any other local employer. It is perfectly true that a tenant, if he is out of debt, is no slave. He is free to move from man to man and place to place. But since everything is run on a personal as well as a business basis, it is up to the tenant to create and to sustain an impression which at worst is not unfavorable. This of course is true in some degree of jobs all over the world, but the case of a man like Burroughs is somewhat special to Burroughs's country:

"I'd be askeered to move any fur place fm Maounvul: I don't know how I'd live. You see I'm knowed here." All three families have moved around some; but none of them has ever moved beyond call of Moundville.

Burroughs has been married eleven years. He farmed for three and got discouraged. He worked in a sawmill for three; got more money. $2 a day; but it cost more to live; and got discouraged. He went back to farming and has been farming the past five years. One year he cleared an encouraging piece of money, he forgets how much, and got him a mule. When he found out how he was coming out the next year he sold the mule and went back on halvers. The most money he ever cleared was $140, in the plow-under year. He made seven bales, more than twice his average, which is around three, and they sold at twelve cents a pound, and he got $25 from the Government on the bale he plowed under. He had $140 clear when all his debts were paid off. The worst year, which was the year before that, he wound up $80 in debt. The last year of which there is a completed record, 1935, he wound up twelve dollars in debt.

The landlord buys his fertilizer in bulk and puts

it against the tenant's account at cost plus interest. That is one strong part of a tenant's debt (once he has paid his rent): the other is the rations money. What that amounts to is come at by agreement of landlord and tenant but depends finally on the landlord. A tenant can, after all, spend every cent he is advanced without notably mussing up the lap of luxury, and every landlord knows that. Some landlords are born tight, others loose with money. Some are sincerely concerned that the tenant does not overdraw and overspend. And some are willing to advance him an amount governed only by an estimate of what his paying-up power will be in the fall. Tenants, so far as their choice goes, have their choice between small possibilities in the spring and large possibilities in the fall, or vice versa. They differ, too. Burroughs has lived on six and on eight dollars a month; this last year it was ten. Fields for several years has taken, for his family of six, seven dollars; and argued it up to nine last year. Tingle, with a wife and seven children, is quite scornful of shortsighted tenants who take it all in rations and have nothing in the fall: his family lives on ten. This money is paid out four and a half months of the year, from the first of March, when the crop is started, through mid-July, when the crop is laid by. Income from the cottonseed varies a little: generally a tenant clears about six dollars on a bale; and a one-mule tenant averages three bales: eighteen dollars or so, to live on during the picking season, between late August and late October.

Fields owns one mule and farms on third and fourth. He has in the past made better money as a halver, but you are ordered around less on third and fourth and he hates to be ordered around. One year back in the War time, when cotton sold for forty cents a pound, he cleared $1,300. Off and on through the twenties he cleared $250 and $300. Even the year before last he cleared $160, but it was a hard winter with a lot of sickness. Some years of course he has cleared next to nothing: a bad crop, or sickness and bills. This last summer his corn was mostly burnt up in the drought; a lot of it didn't even put on the year. Moreover he had heard that the West was burnt up. Corn was already a dollar a bushel and would go higher in the fall and winter. Rather than buy feed for him, he aimed to sell his mule. Burroughs's corn was

better off: it was planted in sandy, moist land, down the slope of the hill.

Tingle's corn was just as bad as Fields's. He planted a lot of late corn, and even by late July it was so sorry that looking at a slope of it from a hundred yards away you couldn't see anything but the blank ground. Of their combined thirty acres Mr. Chris didn't expect fifteen bushels—an exaggeration, but there almost certainly will not be enough to bread the family, let alone feed the mules. He doesn't think of selling the two mules, though: he is an optimist and a progressive, rides a cultivator, and would feel he had gone down a long way in the world if he went back on halvers. Years ago the Tingles were comparatively well-off; they had at one time ten cows and sold the milk. Tingle confidently went in debt $450 for a fine pair of mules. One mule died before its first crop was made; the other died four years later; he nearly died of appendicitis; he nearly died of congestive chills; he had a bad time with dyspepsia of the bowels; his wife got pellagra; now and then children died; he had to go into debt for another pair of mules and became a halvers-hand again. One by one the Tingles, for all their frugality about rations money, have cleared no cash whatever. Last year they came within $125 of paying off their debts. This year they would have done it sure, but for the dry-drouth.

What money they get from cottonseed and clear, or fail to clear, in the Fall, doesn't represent their total income. Between mid-July and late August, and from the end of picking season through to March, the tenant is of no use to the landlord and the landlord is loath to advance money. Unless the tenant has cleared a fair amount (and landlords will tell you that it is extremely rare that they aren't back asking for a loan for Christmas), there are five or six hot weeks in summer and four cold months in winter when he just has to scratch around. If there is wood on the place he has rented he is as a rule welcome to cut it and haul it to town and sell it; a good price is a dollar a load. There are odd jobs of course, sprayed around all through the countryside—very short-term jobs mostly: there are thousands of tenants in the vicinity, all equally in need of work. Last winter Burroughs had so very little work, weeks going by with nothing at all, and nearly nothing to eat, that his landlord advanced him

fifteen dollars or so out of season; an unusual proce-
dure. Last summer, Burroughs was luckier: he and
Tingle both: infinitely more lucky than most people
they knew of. They got jobs bunching logs, for Burroughs's former sawmill employer; snaking them,
with a mule and tongs, into stacks for the wagons,
over at a sawmill about four miles' walk from where
they lived. They got the jobs on condition that they
would quit for nothing, not even picking, and would
stay on as long as there was work to do. Work started
at six-thirty; half hour off for lunch; and ended at five:
ten hours, five and a half days a week, for a dollar
and a quarter a day. Tingle didn't even hire a hand
for the picking: he has a big family. Burroughs had
to hire one either by the day, paying him by the hundred picked, thirty to forty cents, or by the month.
He hired him by the month: room and board and
eight dollars. It was better that way, too, because on
that arrangement a man can't say "you har'd me to
pick cotton": he is a general hired hand, and must
do whatever work comes up. The hired hand was a
single man, and that is a sample of the life of a single
man. That is one good reason why young men of that

class marry young: married, you can rent a farm. And one good reason why they have children thick and fast is that the children are badly needed to help in the fields.

None of the three men is eligible for relief. There is not enough relief money to carry all the widow-women and old people in the country. None of the three is eligible for WPA work either. That too is for people who have no jobs and they, unlike hundreds in that country less fortunate, and scores of total hard-guys and jerktown loafers, and quite some few dozens of the sons of merchants and landowners who want pleasure-money, have jobs. They would be listed as having jobs if they were able to find no work whatever other than their six months of farming per year. Moreover, landlords feel that a man is spoiled for honest work by getting a little money, say $19 a month, in his hands; quite a little more than any landlord wants to let him have: and when there is any prospect of that, plenty of landlords go to the courthouse and guarantee that so-and-so is well taken care of and that the jobs had better be saved for those who need them. A country official can be counted on to understand.

He is, after all, of the landowner's class himself. That is how and why he has the job he has.

None of the heads of the families went to War. Burroughs was too young; the other two were busy raising families and cotton. The draft was just at their ankles when the War ended. Neither of them expresses any profound regret.

Tingle quit voting when the Prohibition went through.

Fields still pays his poll tax. Barring tobacco and occasional drinks, it is his one luxury. He votes only when there is a Republican to vote for. He does that out of independence and spite. At first they made him trouble, of a mild sort, but they just let him go now. It gives him a lot of pleasure.

Burroughs has never registered, much less paid a poll tax.

It has never occurred to any of the women to vote.

They are as oblivious of country and state as of national politics. In fact most people of their sort appear to feel that those structures of Government are irrelevant if not indeed inimical to them. They are amused at the mules who, unlike the Department of Agriculture, knew that cotton should not be stepped on and plowed under, and they are in general glad of the acreage reduction, which is still pretty well held to, because it brought them less work for the same amount of money. But you get up into the poorest levels of the middle class before you run into anyone who will insist that Rowsavelt has done a lot for the poor man.

When the country agent came around to explain the mysteries and rewards of the Triple-A, none of them were at all sure they understood him. They have received checks from time to time, but whether they were fully paid off, they have no clear idea.

One day last August a tombstone drummer spent half an hour approaching Fields. He had no luck but he gave Fields the compliments of the firm, as he left. The compliments were a tinted photograph in a wire frame: that tactfully hale, mildly wardheeler version of the Roosevelt face which was designed to be appropriate to, and which adorns, bars and poolrooms all over the country. The title of the picture was simple: Columbia Marble Works. The whole family looked at it, and said it didn't look hardly a bit like the drummer, and then decided it must be his boss, and finally, because it was a pretty picture, put it on the dresser, where perhaps in the future some Federal Project Publicizer will spot it, get brighteyed, and flash out some fine copy about the Ikon in the Peasant's Hovel.

Fields does, though, know who the President is. The name is Rosenfelt. He has nothing agin him but he wouldn't talk to him, because he is a highfalutin man.

Fields is easily the best-informed and most naturally intelligent of the three.

T*he world is our home. It is also the home of many, many other children, some of whom live in far-away lands. They are our world brothers and sisters.*

Line them up on their front porches, their bodies archaic in their rags as farm bodies are; line them against that grained wood which is their shelter in three rude friezes, and see, one by one, who they are: the Tingles, the Fieldses, the Burroughses.

There are nine Tingles: Frank, Kate, Elizabeth, Flora Bee, Newton, William, Laura Minnie Lee, Sadie, and Ida Ruth. There are six more children, but they are dead.

Frank Tingle is fifty-four. Crepe forehead, monkey eyebrows, slender nearly boneless nose, vermillion gums. A face pleated and lined elaborately as a Japanese mask: its skin the color of corpsemeat. He talks swiftly and continuously as you run downstairs to keep from falling down them; says most things three times over; and clowns a good deal as many sensitive and fearful people do, in self-harmful self-protection. The eyes are shifty and sometimes crazy and never quite successfully crafty: those of a frightened fox with hound blood.

Kate, the mother of thirteen, is forty-nine; delicately made; her skin creamlike where the weather has not got at it. She is smaller than several of her children. Her legs and feet, like those of most women in this country, are beautifully shaped by shoelessness on the earth. Her eyes, which are watchful not at all for herself but for her family, are those of a small animal which expects another kick as a matter of course and which is too numbed to dodge it or even much care. She calls her children "my babies." They call her mama, treat her protectively as they might a deformed child, and love her carelessly and gaily. An old photograph shows her fibre and bearing as a young woman, and perhaps it is the relinquishment of that unusual spirit, under the beating and breakage of the past two decades, that has made her now the most abandoned of all these people: more than any of them, she is lost into some solitary region of her own. She is only half sane.

Mrs. Tingle prefers field work to housework, and her eldest daughters cook most of the meals and take whatever care is taken of the house.

Elizabeth is twenty, and Flora Bee is nineteen. Most girls that age are married and mothers of at least one child. Elizabeth is stocky, and strong at her work as a man: which is just as well, because she does a good deal of man's work. Her features and especially the wry mouth and strong chin and cheeks have something already middle-aged and over-capable about them; her mouth and eyes are desperate, for she has no presentable clothes, and is of white-trash, and sees men seldom, never perhaps on terms of courtship. Flora Bee is more lightly built, a little better-clothed, a little less rooked by work, a little less desperate. She still looks all the way like a young woman. She has a great deal of intuitive graciousness. But she, too, is toward the age when a girl in that country is no longer thought of as marriageable: and the life of a spinster in an impoverished farm family is so ghastly that anything will do for a substitute.

There is about the younger children, about their skin and eyes and hearing and emotions, such an unsettling burn and brilliance as slow starvation can only partially explain. They are emotionally volatile as naphtha; incredibly sensitive to friendliness. You will possibly get the feeling that they carry around in them like the slow burning of sulphur a sexual precocity which their parents fail either to discern or to realize the power and meaning of: and the idea is somewhat borne out in the tone of their play together, and in the eyes of William, who is twelve, and in the wild flirtatiousness of Laura Minnie Lee, who is ten, and in the sullenness and shyness, flared across like burning sedge with exhibitionism, of Sadie, who is

nine, and in the flirting even of Ida Ruth, who is four. A stranger who shows them any friendliness, they meet and surround with the superhuman, millennial sweetness of Polynesians. They sleep mixed, and casual of nakedness. Some idea of that strangeness and obliviousness of the family which has helped to land them in the fix they are in, you may get from their treatment of Ida Ruth. She is possibly the last child they will bring into living, and she is extremely delicate. She dislikes what little food they have but loves chicken and coffee. So, steadily, they have bumped off a long string of chickens to feed her, and she drinks two or three cups of black and parboiled coffee at every meal. Her eyes shine like burning oil and almost continuously she dances with drunkenness.

The Tingles have in fact lost a certain grip on living which the Fields still hold, if feebly and without much interest, and of which the Burroughs, who are a generation younger, are still tenacious. The Tingles no longer think of what life they have in terms of something in the least controllable from season to season or even from day to day: they welter on their living as on water, from one hour to the next, flashing into brief impulse, disorganized and numbed; never quite clear, for instance, who will cook the next meal, or when. Poverty caused their carelessness; their carelessness brings them deeper poverty; disease runs in among them, free as hogs in a garden: and so the intermultiplying goes on, in steady degeneration. That they have been translated into a gayety, a freedom and fearlessness with love, and a sort of sea-floor ultimacy, which the two other families do not enjoy, is definitely worth noting: it is possible to conceive of other paths to salvation which are a little better credit to civilization, and a little less ruinous of human beings.

Bud Fields, Kate Tingle's half-brother, is fifty-nine, and prefers to say he is fifty-four. He is raising his second family. Of his first, the wife and two children are dead. Two sons work halves near Moundville; another is in a CC Camp near Bessemer. His daughter Allie Mae is married to Floyd Burroughs. His daughter Mary, eighteen, has been two years married to an elderly carpenter. Last summer they moved to Mississippi, where they will farm on halves: he couldn't make a living in Tuscaloosa.

When Fields was fifty-one, cancer ate his wife and what money her good management had saved them into the grave. Three years after her death he married again and started farming all over, in the worst of the Depression. He married a young woman named Lily Rogers who had two common-law children by a man back in the hills. He took over one of her children, a little girl named Ruby, and they have had three more: twins, of whom one has died, and a daughter. Mrs. Fields is on her way with another child now.

Fields is slenderly built and no longer strong; a finely shaped head; pale blue eyes whose glitter, like splintered glass, is perhaps a survival of the morphine he was addicted to (and which he broke through whiskey) in the years after his wife's death. He is easily the most intelligent of the three men, skeptical and reflective; and under other auspices would easily have become a dramatic critic or at least a club wit.

His wife Lily comes of casual, strongly sexed, definitively poor people: a combination which automatically brings a bad reputation in that country. Her stepchildren still resent her. She seems to be unconcerned, and unhurt. She is strong as a mule and loves to plow, but her husband disapproves of women plowing.

Ruby has porcelain skin, red hair, lashless redbrown eyes. She is eight years old; observant of people, sophisticated in her deductions, sexually precocious, and deeply attached to her mother. William, who is also called Doogin, is three years old and huge for his age. The mad face of a Jewish lion cub. Deep histrionic and comic intuition and inventiveness. Lillian is a year and a half old. Silent; flesh like biscuit dough; big blank blue eyes and curly mouth set between fat cheeks. The archetypically uninteresting case of baby face.

Miss-Mary, Lily's mother, dresses with an unusual eye for show and color; watches you out of crazy-crafty eyes, and uses language extraordinarily, calling (for instance) babies coons and chicks sings. She looks rather like a derelict member of the Cosmopolitan Club. Since her husband was killed in a crap game she has "made her home" among her relatives. She is the sort of woman the children of Nice people shout after in the street.

F loyd Burroughs and Allie Mae Fields married when he was twenty and she was sixteen; about the average marrying age. They have been married eleven years and had five children. Maggie Lucile, Floyd Junior, Charles Bafford, Martha, and Othel Lee, who is called Squeaky. Martha is dead.

Floyd Burroughs is thirty-one, his features just a little exaggerated beyond that square-chiseled head which the commercial artist Leyendecker sets up as Goodlooking, his build a little stocky, his height medium. He looks bigger than he is because he stoops, as tall men do. He does not look, yet he seems, old enough to be the father of plenty of more softly bred men of his age. His eyes are a clear, ignorant, and somewhere dangerous yellow, quietly studying you. He moves slowly and strongly, in a gait shaped to broken land, and like many people who cannot read or write he handles words with a clumsy economy and beauty, as if they were farm animals drawing open difficult land. He is ordinarily grave, with a ballast rather of profound unrewarded fatigue than of mentality; and gentle, not with the premeditated gentleness of the Christian but with the untraditional gentleness of a large animal. He is capable of murderous anger; and capable also of amusement, over clumsiness embarrassed by pain and over the broader kinds of sexual comedy. He likes to get drunk but can seldom afford to. Down in the creek, whenever he can get company, he swims rambunctiously, turning wild somersaults from the bank and clamping his nose in one hand as he smacks the water. His body, which would otherwise have been very conventionally handsome, is knotted into something else again by the work he has done; and his skin, alarmingly fair beyond the elbows and neck, is cratered and discolored by the food he has eaten and the vermin he has slept with.

Allie Mae is twenty-seven. She inherits the sharp, fine features and the wiry slenderness of her father's people. In no way neurasthenic, she nevertheless takes very little interest in living. Within her natural intelligence you may discern the features of a drowned

intellect. It is easier still to see the steady destruction of an all but beautiful woman; the hard, lean nature of her living has drawn the skin more closely round the bones than need be, and diet, plus the mischance of her own chemistry, has rotted the front teeth out of her upper jaw. Her arms and legs and body are not yet taken out of the shape of a slender comeliness and her walking is joyful to watch, but as she nurses her child you cannot fail to notice how shriveled and knottily veined the breast is; and her hands, when you notice them, are startling: it is as if they were a couple of sizes too large, drawn over what the keen wrists called for.

The appearance of full-blown enigma is infrequent, unexpected and arresting; and it always deserves attention. It happens to reside in the eyes of this eldest child, Lucile, and it is doubly arresting because continuously she uses her eyes to watch into the eyes of other people, quite as calmly as death itself, and as cluelessly, too. Probably she is studying you, without either pity or unkindness, but there is no reason to be sure even of that.

Any definitive mystery is interesting to speculate

over, and thoroughly useless to. These eyes, and whatever is behind them, wear a somewhat more describable creature: a wide forehead; very straight, square-bobbed blond hair that falls over the sweated face; a serene, Scandinavian cast of features, more resolute than conscious resoluteness can be; a sturdily slender, callipygous body, still childish but already subtly blown towards the new dimensions of puberty. She is ten; works in the fields; helps her mother; minds the two smaller children; goes to school and does well there. She still swims in nothing but a pair of aged drawers, but hides her scarcely-discernable breasts within the contraction of her shoulders and upper arms; her mother still makes her dresses halfway to the hips; she is advanced in consciousness to that stage at which a child dislikes its name. Her mother and father are determined to manage it somehow so that she can go all the way through high school. She wants to be a schoolteacher, or a trained nurse.

There is a certain stain of strangeness over Junior, too, in the slantwise way he watches you, and in troubles behind the eyes deeper than he can understand: but some of that can perhaps be explained.

As the first son, he is thought highly of, particularly by his father, and is pretty badly spoiled. As the second child, the young brother of a stronger and more intelligent sister, his self-esteem receives destruction and his jealousy and hatred nourishment at every turn. He compensates in abuse of his own younger and weaker brothers and of animals; and the unconsciousness of his parents allows him a leeway in this, which will probably result, a decade from now, in one of the unpredictable, desperate young men the South is full of. Junior is eight.

Charles is four. If he had genius he would be fortunate, for his psychological soil is rich in fertilizing pain. Since it seems probable that he is of subnormal intelligence his situation is merely pitiable. He is a most remarkably *unnoticeable* child, pale, pretty, weak, and sad. The arrival of his still younger brother forced him out of that strong position of infancy which, thanks to the continuous bullying he receives at Junior's hands, he worse than normally needs. He cries a great deal of the time: so steadily that the crying goes unnoticed, as would the habituate noise of a nearby waterfall; he indulges in baby gibberish, and shows himself capable of normal speech only under the release of marked and affectionate attention; and he is occasionally possessed of rushes of crafty violence against his infant brother, who quite certainly he hates with all his subconscious heart.

"The reason why Squeaky is so cute is he's so little," his aunt Mary says. He is a few months short of two years old. A year ago last summer he quit growing; that summer's dresses still fit him tidily. Lively, clownish and amiable, shining with dwarfish vivacity, trotting around on shriveled hind quarters, he inspires sudden love in those whose crippled insides have no need to kill or torture him.

CHAPTER 2

Shelter

The land Floyd Burroughs has rented is broken among woods and upon the falling shapes of the hill into stripe and patches. Except for a couple of acres of red land, pretty well uphill behind the house, it is all sandy. He has about twenty-one acres in cultivation: two acres in cotton up on the hill (pronounced heel): about two more dropping from the left of the house to the woods; five more on the fall of land out in front of his house, and out along the ruined road to the right, three more: a little less than twelve acres in cotton. There is an acre in corn out to the left of the house on the far side of a strip of woods; one and a half acres out in front; and on the strips of land out the road nearly four more; and out in the same road, little patches in peanuts and potatoes and watermelon, and a quarter of an acre of sorghum cane. The land Fields and Tingle farm, up on the crest of the hill, rolls more gently and is less broken up. It is all red land. Fields plants about the same amount of cotton, a little more corn, a little less of everything else than Burroughs; Tingle just about twice as much, in the same proportions, and a little bit of hay. They all plant peas in their cornrows.

About in the middle of its land as among tough distorted petals the Burroughs house stands, about halfway down one hill, facing across its bare stumpy yard (in which blooms one small pink planted flower) that westward face of the hill which smothers in woods and ends in the wandering of a coffee-colored and malarious creek. Squared around the bare hard dirt back of the house are the three outbuildings: the henroost, the smokehouse, the combination stall, hogpen, cottonhouse, corncrib. (Nothing is smoked in the smokehouse: it affords storage for farm tools, sorghum, and shoes and junk too old for use but never to be thrown away.) These buildings could all but be pushed flat by one man who tried hard.

There is no backhouse. Out to the left of the house, where summer cotton offers concealment, there is a specifically fertile patch on which Burroughs did not bother to waste professional fertilizer. Jokes about mail order catalogues are not in order, because people with so little money do not order by mail. They buy what they can when they can at the local stores, and for sanitary purposes they use leaves, sticks and corncobs.

Out to the right of the house, caught within palings against the hunger and damage of the animals, is a patch of land a little bigger than a tennis court: this is the garden. Floyd breaks the land: the rest is his wife's business. Out of paper seed-packets she plants two crops a year: a summer crop of vegetables, a winter crop of collards and turnips.

Beyond the garden and a little uphill, about a hundred and fifty yards from the house and just within the sudden cool and darkness of trees, is the water supply: a small but steady spring, shored up in wood. A lardpail, rusted black and split at the edges, hangs beside it on an upright stick: a crock of butter, a jar of milk, stand in the water. The spring is not so deeply cowled beneath the hill that the water is cold and nervy: it is about the temper of faucet water, and it tastes sad on the mouth.

Ten feet or so below the spring the water is held up again, beside one of those thick and black iron kettles in which farm people a shade more primitive make soap. There is also a washboard, homemade out of a piece of thick pine plank, and here every Wednesday in fair weather Mrs. Burroughs and Lucile do the laundry. (The Fields and Tingles, with a less convenient water supply and less consciousness of dirt, launder less frequently.)

It is a four-room house: two rooms on either side of a roofed hallway open to the porch on one end, the hard dirt yard on the other. The porch is made of oak so stout it still has a thick hair of splinters. The rest of the house is entirely of pine, stitched with nails into as rude a garment against the hostile year as a human family can wear. Four rooms: more spacious a house than the average. Three of the rooms are quite good-sized, twelve by fifteen feet; and the kitchen is half that size. One of the rooms, however, is uninhabitable: on two sides there is a wide gap between eaves and wall, and on the hallway side several courses of weatherboard have been omitted between the height of the wall and the tall peak of the roof: and there is no ceiling. In this room are stored corn, dried peas, dried peaches, jellies, and canned food, for the winter. The opposite room is semihabitable: no ceiling, the same big gap at the eaves. There is a bed there: no space for it in the bedroom, which already has two: and sometimes the children try sleeping there. On the whole, though, they prefer their pallets on the bedroom floor. These rooms are not good for living because they are so wide open to cold by winter, to anopheles mosquitoes in the spring and summer, and to wet weather in all times of year. To make the roof tight would be no job of patching but of completely relaying the half-inch thick pine shingles. Even the walls are insecure against cold and against slanted storms, though the worst rifts have been papered, or caulked with rags or cotton. Stand there in the darkness of daytime and through walls and roof the sunlight will reach at you in slashes and innumerable stars. The bedroom is ceiled, and one of its windows is screened and can be opened at night. The ceiling leaks only in really wet weather, and badly in only three places. There are two windows to each room, with wooden shutters. Those in the storeroom are nailed shut; those in the opposite room are seldom opened; of those in the bedroom only the screened is ever opened (and the door is buttoned shut at night). The kitchen windows are glazed; and Floyd has roofed the kitchen with corrugated tin. The odor of the house is a complex of pinewood, woodsmoke, pork, lardsmoke, corn, lampsmoke, and sweat, and the sweat is a distillation chiefly of corn and lard and pork. Flesh stewed in these odors year after year gets beyond the reach of bathing; the odor stands out of the fibers of newlaundered clothes.

The pinewood, its grain stormplaned, stormsilvered, and sharp in the eye as razors, is lovelier than watered silk; a fact which is not appreciated by those whose bare feet smooth its floors and whose bodies revolve through living among the frail cards it lifts against the weather, and whose lives are trapped in it.

The notable thing about the house, though, is its bareness, which is as much more bare than nakedness as bone: and the bareness is intensified not only by the lack of furniture but by the rigorous cleanliness of the floors.

The house was totally bare, of course, when the

Burroughs moved in. No landlord furnishes furniture. In the course of living at all, though, even without money to speak of, there is a slow but certain accumulation of possessions: some of them, indeed, are useless and decorative. There are salient items:

In the front room (semihabitable): one iron bed, drooping springs, two thin mattresses stuffed with cotton, cotton sheets whose texture of coarseness is that of an unwashed floursack, a quilt, a mercerized salmon-colored spread. A dresser with drawers whose handles are missing and a mirror whose quicksilver is corrupting. A Conquest sewing machine. A small table, stuffed drawer (old clothes) jammed against the never used fireplace. Under the sewing machine, the square glass base of a defunct lamp. A settee, "rustically" bent out of withes from which the bark has not been cleaned. A trunk, low, short, and narrow, its rusted tin skin pressed into floral patterns and studded with roundhead nails.

In the bedroom: two iron beds; mattresses, sheets, and quilts as above. Thin cotton-stuffed pallets for the children, rolled up during the day, in the closet. A small table, for the lamp when it is transferred from

the kitchen for undressing just after supper. A twelve-gauge shotgun, slung from two forked sticks above Burroughs's bed. In a closet: miscellaneous clean and dirty clothes, and quilts. Quilts enough to keep warm under in winter except perhaps in really cold nights.

In the kitchen: a small range. A woodbox. A small earthenware churn. A heavy black iron pot. Black breadpans. A couple of stewpots. A dishpan. A fifty-pound lard tin, containing meal and covered with a wire sieve. A table, covered with worn patterned oilcloth. Skillets, their handles stuck in cracks in the wall. A quite modern safe (cupboard) with a metal-lined bin for flour. Dishes of miscellaneous size and pattern, which are sufficient because the children use bowls or saucers. Knives, forks, and spoons of a metal which imparts its taste to all the food you eat. The stainless steel forks and two stainless steel knives, with black wood handles. A bench. A sealoil lamp. A bucket on a shelf.

In the hallway, by the kitchen door: an oilcloth covered shelf, waist-high, supporting a bucket, a soaptray, and a small enameled basin. From a nail, a towel: half a floursack. The soap is sometimes toilet, sometimes kitchen, sometimes nil. The Burroughs are unusually cleanly. Not only do they wash their faces, and their arms to the elbow, before every meal, as all farm people do: one by one on their way to bed, in a basin for that single purpose, they wash their feet. It is very seldom that the whole body is washed: when they go to the creek, though, for their infrequent swims, they take along soap. Two more things may as well be noted here: they sleep all in one room, and there is no such thing as privacy, by day or by night; and on the other hand they have uncommon physical modesty.

In the walls of the bedroom and of the front room, somewhat at random, are driven nails. Here and there, clothes hang from them.

On the walls are pasted or tacked such items as these: a calendar advertising Peters Shoes, depicting a pretty girl in a red hat, cuddling red flowers. Title: Cherie. Subtitle (written twice, in pencil): Lucile.

A tinted photograph of a neat, new-overalled, clean country boy fishing. Title: Fishin'. Torn from a child's book, costume pictures in furry colors illustrating, as you might expect them to be illustrated, these titles: The Harper Was Happier Than a King as He Sat by His Own Fireside. She Took the Little Prince in Her Arms and Kissed Him. Slung by its chain from a nail: a cheap locket depicting Jesus Christ and the Blessed Virgin, with their respective hearts exposed. Torn from a tin can: a strip of bright red paper sporting a white fish and bearing the legend: Salomar Extra Quality Mackerel. On the mantel: twin iridescent vases. Between them: a saucer of pressed milky glass. On a table: a green glass bowl in which sits a white glass swan. On the dresser: a broken china rabbit; a china bulldog and litter of china pups—Lucile was given them last Christmas. (Folded away for use year after year are the gaycolored, now faded papers in which gifts are wrapped.) For one of the mantels Mrs. Burroughs designed out of white tissue one of those scissored stretches of paper lace which children so enjoy making. But she has just about given up trying to make the house pretty.

There are also four straight hickory-bottom chairs, a "rustic" straight chair, and a "rustic" rocker. They are moved around as needed. The price of a straight chair is a dollar and a half.

There are easy-payment stores in Tuscaloosa, which do a good business with people as poor as the Burroughs but less foresighted. More generally, furniture is got at when a family diminishes by death or marriage, or through a barter of needs: everyone, after all, always needs something. One of the beds the Fields got will give an idea of prices: it cost a dollar and a quarter, and it is so crippled they have had to nail the head into the wall to keep it from collapsing.

Burroughs has some animals, too: a heavy yellow rooster with a fierce eye and an androgynous voice; a clutter of obese hens whose bodies end dirtily, like a sheaf of barley left out in the rain; a number of neat broilers, and a few quilty, half-dressed chicks. A couple of guineas whose small painted heads and fluent bodies thread these surroundings like a dream. A sad, darkbrown, middlesized dog named Rowdy who, though he looks like André Gide, is as intensely American a type of dog as Burroughs is a man. Two longlegged, rusty young hogs for which Burroughs paid his landlord $9 when they were shoats. A cow, tethered from spot to spot in the green stretches, for which Burroughs gave a fifty-dollar grafanoler. Her calf. A small white pup named Sipco. A half-grown, reptilian black cat named Nigger. A nameless adolescent tiger-cat, that just took up with them. A rented mule, which is on hand only between March and July and during the picking season. In a way, the whole place is possessed by animals. Wasps whine threadily from their nest under the hot peak of the roof; rats skitter and thump and gnaw, and fight the cats; the hens tread the bare floors on horny feet; sharpen their bills on the boards, their eyes blue with autoeroticism; the broilers dab and thud at the mealy dung which the pup and, weightily, the youngest child, have delivered about the floor; the dogs and cats are gathered in by the odor of food among the bare feet under the kitchen table, Rowdy apologizing for getting his ribs kicked in, perfectly in that manner which has moved man to call the dog his best friend.

The Burroughs have been working for Fletcher Powers only for a year. For three years before that they worked for the Tidmore brothers, and they lived in the house the Fields family now occupies. It is a less spacious house: smaller rooms, and only three of them. Half the house is constructed in a way more characteristic of that country, perhaps, than any other: the walls are vertical planks a foot wide, with laths tacked on the lengths of the cracks. The Fieldses' windows are glazed and curtained. The stove has supported two families and it is assumed that the rigors of another moving will end its usefulness. There is an iron ice cream chair with a homemade seat of new pine. There is a tin-framed mirror over which certain fanciers of the antique would have nocturnal emissions. There is a pot of tinstemmed paper flowers. On the bedroom wall is a blunt officer's sword in a rusted scabbard: it was supposedly used by an ancestor of the present Mrs. Fields. On another wall is a picture, from some inexplicable magazine, of little Barbara Drake and of John B. Drake III of Chicago, who at four or five has already achieved the poisonous expression which in due time may serve to abash traffic officers, panhandlers, and even the legal managers of jilted showgirls. Caption: The Little Drakes. The water supply is a spring, sixty feet down the steep clay bank out back. No one who uses the spring seems to have very good health. The water-getting contraption is a lazyboy: a windlass, a stoneballasted bucket on a wire, a frayed rope innumerably broken. You have to wind with one hand and guard with the other to get the bucket uphill. There is also a cow named Mooly who would as soon kill the young ones as not and who, one day last winter, knocked Mrs. Fields down and stomped on her, cutting her shins badly and bruising her from head to foot. There is also a red hog, so hungry it fumbles, with its jaws, at the tail of a kitten too dizzy with hunger to move.

The Tingles live in what was once a farmhouse. There is a shade tree, and a flowering bush out of the bare yard. There are three rooms on one side of the house, like a dumbbell flat: there is another across the open hallway. The windows are glazed, screenless, closed at night. The house is extremely dark, partly with the set of the windows, partly with the absorption of smoke, and partly with a rich patine of grease and dirt so labored into its once whitewashed surface that sweeping and scrubbing affect it as lightly as if it were iron. The walls are heavily decorated with calendars and other ads. The kitchen table and its oilcloth have absorbed grease and corn and cornsweat to a degree which extends a globe of nausea thick and clinging as oil. The bedding, the clothing, and the people are insanely dirty. The drinking and cooking water are caught off the roof and stored in a cistern. How sound its walls are is of some importance because a hole in the porch, not far away, is used for nocturnal convenience. This cistern water must be used sparingly: even so it sometimes runs dry; did last summer. The laundry is done at the spring down behind Fields's house, a third of a mile and a steep hill away. So the laundry is done seldom. There are dogs, Queenie and Sport, very lean and hungry but fatted as compared to the trembling back kitten, whose skin is ridged raw along the bones. There are roosters named Bud and Floyd; hens named Lily and Alliemae; a cat named Hazel who is big enough to get what food she needs. Late last summer the Tingles blew themselves to a new washbasin. Before that they had been washing in a hub cap. Tingle has boasted, laughingly, that he has not bought a bar of soap in five years: but that is doubtless an exaggeration.

CHAPTER 3

Food

All a human being needs to live on is food, clothing, and shelter. And, to a man anyhow who must do a lot of hard work; to a woman who must do likewise and carry a child during the fourth to half her mature existence; and to children whose Little Bodies Need Building, perhaps the least dispensable of the three is food.

It is therefore a pleasure to be able to report that the Burroughs and their neighbors can virtually always count on three meals a day, except perhaps during those four hard winter months when, after all, no one in their position can be sure of anything. But let us take not merely an average day but a day better than average, when the meals are three and square: a day in full summer, at the Burroughses, where the cooking is cleanest.

Breakfast begins at about four, by lamplight

which pales as it proceeds. It is a very important meal, particularly to Floyd, because he has the height of an increasingly hot morning to climb, and his morning is eight hours long. There is always coffee: coalblack, crudely bitter, silty, scorching hot. There is nearly always biscuit, fresh-baked and likewise hot, and very heavy. When there isn't biscuit there is warmed over cornbread. There is fry more often than not: a saucer floating, in their grease, six or eight small patches of salt pork, fat almost untainted by any hint of pink fiber. Often, too, there are eggs; plenty when there are any; and whenever there are eggs they are fried; and whenever they are fried they are fried hard as yellow-white stones. Always there is sorghum and, in the summer, fresh unsalted butter. Floyd eats four or five big biscuits, three or four eggs, two or three pieces of the fry, and big helpings of the grease and sorghum, which he mixes with his spoon and takes up on his biscuit. He drinks three or four cups of the coffee, without sugar (though there is sugar), out of his saucer. Towards the end of his breakfast, Allie Mae sits down to hers, and their children come in, by order of age, stiff with sleep. Everyone is quiet at breakfast, around the lamp under the increasing light: there is a formal quality about it, as about the silent meals in monasteries.

Lucile and her mother eat the normal foods, less of them than Floyd does: the three boys eat what the little children eat. Junior and Charles each have a piece of the fry, if there is any left, and maybe half an egg, and a big glass of the buttermilk, and a lot of biscuit, which Floyd hands them stuck on his fork. But the fry and egg are adult foods, to which they are being broken in. Mainly their meal is this: they put two or three spoonsful of sugar in the middle of their saucers, pour on sorghum out of the Mason jar, and get helped to pork grease. This they mix thoroughly with the spoon and take up on their biscuits. The baby meanwhile has had prepared for him a miniature edition of this and a bowl of bread broken in buttermilk. He stands up to it on the bench the three boys use, hanging his round paunch over the china like a Jefferson Day banquet speaker, revolving his bright glance, and going through the seldom completed gestures of eating, jerkily yet gracefully, like a faulty clockwork doll unwinding. What he actually lives on he gets of his mother, many times during the day. Meanwhile the flies are wakening more and more thickly and meanwhile, too, the dogs and cats have assembled under the table, in postures which would do honor to any Bethlehem stable painting of the Holy Family. The dogs are fed at length—mainly on cornbread. Nobody likes the cats or ever pays them any sort of attention; they have to fend for themselves. As the meal disorganizes, Nigger flows up on the bench, insinuates his snaky skull and grabs what he can. He and his companion make it up on fast lizards, fat rats, and an occasional snake.

Floyd has left before it is all over. He is working in the fields, or working at the sawmill, or looking for work. During chopping time, Allie Mae and Lucile and Junior work all day with him; during the picking season, Charles helps, too. And even in the emptier times of year there is work for his family, and the whole weight of living is in work: clearing the table, washing the dishes, milking the cow, churning, sweeping the floors, scrubbing them once or twice a week, cultivating the garden, shifting the cow to fresh feeding, breaking off corntops, gathering vegetables, drying peaches, peas, and beans, canning, making jelly, laundering, mending clothes, making clothes, minding the children, slopping the hogs: plenty of work. It is done steadily, at a quiet place, and though there is a lot of it there is also a good deal of leisure: a leisure which, as a rhythm of the day, is a sliding into blank and glassy quiet of water: a space in the hot middle of the morning, another in the afternoon, when a woman is just sitting, in the blue shade of the porch next the white edge of heat, with all her joints disengaged and her eyes nearly as bare as a child's; while her baby sleeps on the floor, beneath a flyswarmed floursack, and her children convolve in any chance stage between heat-enchanted silence and rampant cruelty against each other or the animals. It is the time of morning when Mrs. Tingle comes in gray-faced and gasping from the sunlight among the dark green shadows of her house, falls into a chair, wipes her delicate reeking head on her skirt and, reviving a little, from between lip-pressing fingers squirts snuff-water over the heads of her children into the fireplace. There is always more talk among the Tingles than elsewhere: someone has always been hurt, or is feeling poorly, or has done something laughable. In season, in the middle of the morning, a melon is cut and divided and everyone eats by wet hand or knife while the hens stab at the slippery seeds. Everyone is hungry by that time of morning, and the melon gives a better illusion of fulness than the cold cornbread on which, in other times of year, the children fill up. Blown up with soda as it is, the melon is also liable to loosen the bowels and to weaken and sicken in general, but one becomes accustomed to that.

Dinner is usually about noon; no set time.* The children have gathered it out of the garden, and Allie Mae has cooked it and possibly shown Lucile something about cooking, a craft as traditional from mother to daughter and as hermetically sealed against innovation as the patterns in Persian rugs used to be. The stove and the tin roof together make the small kitchen so hot, at dinner time, that the sweat starts out and streams all over your body the instant you come in the door, and all through the meal the

*Though each family has a lowprice alarm clock and as a rule keeps it wound and is respectful of it, the clock is almost invariably an hour or two fast or slow, and they are innocent of any time except the sun's.

oilcloth is slippery as a rink under your bare forearms. The animals are there, in their scheduled dancelike places and postures; and the flies are there, a whole drowsing fog of them, struggling and letching on the food, hanging from the mouths and the plastered cheeks of the children, vibrating to death in the buttermilk.

The constants for the middle of the day are cornbread, peas, and molasses. The peas are not the green ones you may be thinking of, which are rarely raised and are called English peas: these are field peas, small, oval, colored a dirty mauve. They are very dense, not unlike some large version of the lentil which, by the way, is a staple of the French peasant. They are boiled three hours, in water heavily "seasoned" with lard. The cornbread is turned out from the pan, a footlong slab, generally milkless and eggless; so hot it burns your fingers as you break off your piece, appetizing, and as heavy as wet concrete. The sorghum is just as usual: a sour, heavy, heady, black taste. There is also, usually, some other vegetable: boiled potato, fried okra, thin stewed tomato, boiled corn, butterbeans, stringbeans: vote for one or, quite seldom, two. The stewed tomato is called soup: so is any mixture of two boiled vegetables. The okra is fried with a thick crumbing of yesterday's cornbread. Everything is cooked with lard and mulled in a puddle of sorghum; the juices are sopped up in crumbed bread; the plate is wiped with a crust. The three younger children eat small helpings of this material; a lot of bread and sorghum; a glass of buttermilk. There is no meat.

Supper is dinner warmed over, plus a fresh batch of biscuit, plus sometimes jelly or jam or preserves, plus sometimes meat: pieced out, perhaps, with another vegetable if dinner was overeaten. Though the meal is always eaten by lamplight, the day still makes it pale. Before supper is over, Junior and Charles have slid from their bench and flopped on the floor like dogs, dead asleep. Floyd sits in the hallway, heavy with daylight, smoking, while his wife and daughter clear the table and wash the dishes. His bare feet like roots draw comfort from the gritty floor. When Allie Mae and Lucile are done they will maybe sit with him a few minutes, the two adults windlassing out of the deep wells of their fatigues their gently low voices, communicating little about nothing, with long falls of silence. Generally, though, they are too tired. The lamp is transferred to the bedroom. One by one, in the basin reserved for that purpose, they wash their feet; by sexes and with modesty, they retire into that room where six sleep in no privacy, and undress. The wife and daughter change into cotton shifts the respective ruin and april of their flesh, only seventeen years apart; they turn their heads away as Floyd comes last, bringing the bucket and dipper, buttons the door, and takes from the nail beside speech, sometimes with a weaving of goodnights and then blank silence, they are asleep, generally, before the last daylight is lost out of the air. Frogs, the dark, take over with noise the dampened and lowbreathing world, but upon this house and the effigies within it, and upon each of a million square houses of that country, there is inviolable silence. A man may wake, coughing in darkness; a child may cry, and be quieted; on the porch, a dog may burst up bellowing from a nightmare and set ten miles of country echoing with his kind: yet these are merely enhancements of a most profound and noble silence: that silence peculiar to the deathlike resting,

LUCILE BURROUGHS PICKING

under the seaweight of deep country night, of people who work.

That is supper; and three square meals a day; and that is the shape of a day; strung between two flowerings of a lamp; slung from its meals as from three thick wood pegs; and mostly work; and the leisure mindless.

Next day, breakfast is this: black coffee, fried eggs, hot biscuit, butter, fry, sorghum; buttermilk for the children. Dinner is this: peas, cornbread, sorghum. Some one of a half dozen vegetables; buttermilk for the children. Supper is this: dinner warmed over, plus maybe meat, plus maybe another vegetable; buttermilk for the children.

The day after that, breakfast is just the same. So is dinner. So is supper.

Two weeks from now, a chicken may be killed and fried, or boiled with dumplings.

Once in a great while there is cake: a plain sponge cake with cocoa-chocolate frosting. Or a cocoa-chocolate pudding. Or a sweetpotato pie. Or a can of salmon.

There are two appletrees. Their yield is small,

sour and negligible: good only for betweenmeals and bellyaches.

There are three or four peachtrees; one was blown down last summer. During the summer the small sweet peaches are stoned and put on the tin roof to dry. Stews and occasional pies are made of them. Peas are dried. Beans are dried. Some figs are got by barter, and preserved. Peaches, beans, butterbeans, tomatoes, are put up in jars. Berries come ripe during a time when everyone's help is needed in the fields; but so much as there has been time for, they are put up in stews or jams or jellies.

Early every spring, they buy a shoat or two. Every September they begin to fatten them on corn. Late every fall they knock them on the head with the flat of an axe, hang them up by their hind feet, slit their throats, let them drain, cut them up, and put them down in salt: meat for the winter. It is seldom a family can afford to carry a hog over to the next year, when his meat might really amount to something: generally he is only eight months old when he is killed. He doesn't by any means last them out the winter. Burroughs's two hogs won't last them out for that matter unless they go very easy on the meat and lard. They have more meat in winter than in summer, though, because in summer they have to buy it.

During the winter, then, there is salt pork. There are preserves and jams. There are canned vegetables. There are dried peaches and beans and peas. There are peanuts. There is, if the season was normal, enough cornmeal to bread them. How much of everything else there is depends on several things: the providence of the woman, the size of the garden, the chance of the season, the size, appetite, and self-control of the family. Plenty of women are far less foresighted than Mrs. Burroughs; plenty plant little, more monotonously, and can much less in less variety, or none. No gardens are large. Much canned-goods spoils, as in the case of Mrs. Fields, for lack of the half dollar it would take to buy new rubbers and new tight leads for the jars. Unbridled hunger by summer means less to put up for the winter; by winter, less to satisfy it that much sooner. The tenant's life is a mirrormaze of such little choices between two losses. The winter diet of a more normal family than the Burroughses is reduced to winter greens and roots, peas, cornbread, and sorghum: and even that can fail. Burroughs even, with his corn in moist sandy land, is sure to have to buy it for bread this winter, at at least a dollar a bushel for ungristed corn: Fields and Tingle have virtually no corn at all, and a poor crop of peas.

Add on food:

One morning Lily Fields's mother came trudging back from a visit, bringing a letter from a relative (letters go by hand, seldom by mail). Her greeting from down the road was "Kill the cat, compny's acomin."

It is not likely that cats are often killed, even for Christmas dinner, but collectors of Americana are welcome to add it under Section 7G: Sardonic Humor with a Certain Grim Underlying Reality.

This is worth adding, too, as indicative of the strength of custom and the asininity of deploying the totally unintuitive Nicegirl type of dietician who is customarily sent out to bring the gospel to these women:

Far from being able to afford the pure hoglard needed for good "seasoning" of everything that goes into the face, Mrs. Fields often can't even afford the "compound." In that case she jist has to git along the best way she can on butter.

That is all. The food at the Fieldses' is what land-owners and tenants unite in describing as good plain country food, a shade more monotonous and several shades less clean than at the Burroughs'.

The Tingles have a harder time. Less money per head accounts for their food in part; a lack of any sense of system, and an all but total loss of conscious-ness of dirt, accounts for it the rest of the way. They raise virtually nothing in their garden of that mild ar-ray which gives at least a little variety to the other two tables; they can only peaches and —— for the winter: things dry up on them in their garden, or choke under the weeds. It comes down to just about this: coffee, buttermilk, butter, sorghum, less than half as much pork per head as in the other two families; cornbread, fieldpeas, sweet potatoes; biscuit; most of it informed with lard that somehow always manages to be rancid. All this cooked in pots and eaten off china and "silver" that has been cleaned infrequently and with still less frequent thoroughness; off a table whose odors have been spoken of; and among a steady black drowse and the affection of flies. One who isn't used to this food and who brings a bite of it towards his mouth, finds every muscle and tissue from navel to epiglottis closing and wrestling against it. They are used to it of course, and that doubtless makes everything all right. Most of them eat with good appetite. As Tingle says: "We're regular meat *eat*ers. No knickknacks, no borl nothn. Give me meat and biscuit three times a day year round and I'll lof for ye ever day the sun shines." Mrs. Tingle can't eat meat, though. She eats biscuit two times *ever* day, because she needs to fill up, but it hurts her. "Nor butter neither. Molasses: I like them but I can't eat." She can eat mush, or soup. She likes turnip soup, though people do say you might as well to eat the booger man as to drink his blood. Once in a while she gets back to the stove and makes mushmelon cake, and last Christmas she made them a banana cake. It would warm the cockles and, very possibly, the ventricles of any good Dickensian to see how delightedly Newton, on those happy occasions when another chicken is killed, tackles the gold bone feet.

But getting back to the supernormalcy of the Burroughs, let us make a last checkup on food.

Outside of an occasional chicken, a dependable part of whose diet has been human excrement, there is never any meat except pork, and never any pork except salt pork, and never more than a dab of that at a time, and often enough not even a dab.

There is virtually never any sweet milk even for the children, because that would be a waste of good butter.

There is very seldom any fish. When there is, it is canned fish.

Of the vegetables which began life green, there are few. They are cooked with pork when there is pork to spare; they are cooked in lard when there isn't; they are at all times cooked far beyond greenness to a deep olivecolored death.

Everything, in fact, fried, boiled, or baked, is heavily seasoned with lard, and flows lard from every pore. So, after even a meal or two, do you.

Between thirty and forty per cent of all the food taken into the body is corn. To mention merely the doubtless negligible esthetic angle on this, two weeks of corneating blackens the never-brushed teeth and draws over each tooth a peculiarly thick and odiferous woolen sock of tartar.

Quite certainly twenty per cent of the rest of the food is field peas.

All the food is doubleseasoned with sorghum, which blinds its monotony with a more powerful monotony, and loosens the bowels.

Through five months of fall, winter, and early spring this fare is diminished to canned and dried foods cheered only by winter greens which, again, are cooked to the texture of shoetongues.

It is only fair to observe of this food as of much about their living that they "like" it—prefer it, indeed, by some odd chance, to things which have never entered their experience: and that a good deal must be explained less in terms of their present particular situation as cotton tenants than in terms of ignorance, slovenliness, and small-farm tradition all over that country. And it is quite as fair to observe that ignorance and slovenliness and the tradition itself are the inevitable products of just one thing: poverty. The music can go all sorts of places but it comes out here.

And now finally realize, insofar as that is vicariously possible, that this steady, brutal bastinado of the bowels and belly and brain goes on every few hours three times a day (when there is food at all, that is) for exactly as long as life lasts. Consider seriously the favorableness of this food as a diet for an unborn and for a suckling infant; for a child; for an adolescent; for an adult: and consider seriously whether it is not remarkable to the point of nausea that a plant nurtured in such soil should manage to live not in any full health nor in any fulfillment of its form, but at all.

The human organism, however, is remarkably tenacious of life, and miraculously adapted to it. In the course of adapting, it may be forced to sacrifice a few side-issues, such as the capability of thinking, of feeling emotion, or of discerning any possibilities of joy or goodness in living: but it lives.

Twenty-six thousand feet up the cols of Everest, a long way beyond the staying power of plants, pale spiders have been found, who subsist on nothing more discernible than air. Apparently they also reproduce their kind. What else they do with their time and, for that matter, why, no one has yet made out.

CHAPTER 4
Clothing

Some pretty silly attitudes could be and have been struck over the subject of clothes: such as reproaching society for the fact that tenant farmers do not plow in swallowtails. The fact remains, however, that clothes are powerfully significant psychologically and socially: in every garment you see there is a badge and division of class as distinct as any uniform could effect and far more subtly exact; and a human being is shaped by the clothes he wears quite as much as by the amount of money he is accustomed to feel the presence, or lack thereof, in his pocket; and as the world is today the future of a marriageable girl, for instance, can be profoundly influenced by what clothes she can or cannot wear.

Another fact to bear in mind is that "ugly" and "humble" clothes, shaped to their context, can like

the people who wear them have an extraordinary dignity and beauty: and that this fact in turn is heavily qualified by considerations such as those mentioned above.

If in the illustrations and the following inventory you are surprised at the number of figured prints and "store" clothes and the number of garments in general, remember two things: that in a society steeped to the teeth in the fears and coercions of snobbery every class inclines to be emulous of the one next "above" it; and that poor people, particularly farmers, never throw anything away that has a conceivable ounce of usefulness left in it.

All right: any summer weekday, drop in on the Burroughses, and see what they are wearing.

Burroughs will be wearing overalls, pronounced overhalls, and a blue workshirt. Heavy shoes if he is at work; none if he is resting. On his head will be not the routine broadbrimmed straw (on which in fact one farmer in two creates a variant), but a bold-striped, square-visored ship cap. He has three or four changes of work clothes, and puts on a clean outfit every Monday morning or Saturday noon. They are in several stages of wear: none of them are new, and won't be till fall, when and if there is money. The elder of them are fainted by sweat and sun to a subtle and very beautiful blue. They become frail with sweating and tear against the active body. Then they are stitched and later patched. Then stitches and patches are added over those; until at length whole sections of a garment, particularly round the swing and crest of the shoulders, contain virtually nothing of the original cloth but are one fabric of stitches and patches, as intricate and delicate as the feather cloak of a Toltec prince. This color and this richness of mending, of course, are characteristic of all old clothes in that country.

Saturday morning if there is time, and if not, then certainly on Sunday, Burroughs shaves. When he is unemployed he shaves twice a week. His equipment is a brokenhandled mug with rosebuds wreathing it, a sliver of toilet soap, a rundown tencent varnish brush, a straight razor, a strop made of an old belt, and a clear cheap mirror in a wire frame. Like all country men, he looks bashful and naked after he has shaved.

For the Saturday trip to Moundville he will dress either in the less ruined of his work clothes or in his Sunday clothes. These are the Sunday clothes: A light unionsuit. A pair of hard, dollar-and-a-half, cotton-wool store pants. A pair of fancy-patterned tencent mercerized socks, strung over the fistlike calves, one with a garter of pink and the other of green, scrap gingham. Black cheap dress shoes, streaked with rainy clay. A white or striped cotton shirt, detachable collar; collar detached. A gold-gray felt hat, of which his head and hands are still shy. The lining of the hat and the band, and the bright insole of the shoes, will be scarcely blemished for years to come.

He doesn't like coats. What he wants to get is a pullover sweater.

Allie Mae is barefooted, most likely, though if she has had warning she will have put on the ruined oxfords her husband's Sunday shoes superseded, and will quickly remove the sunbonnet she works in. (No more handsome headgear has ever been evolved, but it is "oldfashioned," like snuff-dipping.) Her dress, whichever one it may be, began as a cheap cotton print for best and has been washed, worn, sunned,

BUD FIELDS AND HIS FAMILY AT HOME

FLOYD BURROUGHS AND TINGLE CHILDREN

FLOYD BURROUGHS, SHARECROPPER

ALLIE MAE BURROUGHS

HOUSE OF BUD FIELDS

CORNER OF KITCHEN

PART OF BURROUGHS' COTTON

COUNTY SEAT

and sweated into something more faint and sad and finelooking. She has made it herself, like most of the other clothes. It is cut perfectly straight, longskirted, without decoration, loost at the breast for nursing. For town or Sunday, she puts on, newlaundered, one of the two or three dresses she would conceivably wear except at home; a fragile lavender straw hat, small and misshapen and worn on her shy graven head with sorrowful, clumsy, and ridiculous grace; black flatheeled slippers; and sometimes cotton stockings. Never worn, and probably never to be thrown out, are two other hats. One is a formerly Snappy red felt, impaled aslant with a stripped white quill. The other is a great-brimmed, triumphal affair, homemade out of scraps of cheap gold plush, cheap iridescent brocade, and cheap braid; irrevocably moldered and busted. It is a hat she cannot have had the heart to wear since she was sixteen and a bride: in the short while before, like every bride of her kind, she was drawn into the rollers in good earnest, and methodically defaced among them.

Speaking generally as well as of the Burroughses, the work clothes of the grown people become them as their own skins do. In their Good clothes they look stiff and shy, like orphans at a party.

Lucile's mother dresses her carefully in the idiom of the little girl she is ceasing to be, and a "respectable" little girl at that: she will never have to wear what Ruby, far less the Tingle children, wear, and the psychological imprint is going to be strong on her, and not entirely fortunate. Excepting one or two flimsy skirts of sheeting cotton she wears dresses made of store cloth, of gay though faded colors, and with some style of cut, sashed, and ruched out behind like a pulley: and beneath, the floursack clout which appears to be the standard lingerie in that country. She and the other children are customarily barefooted from early spring through the fall and, with all serious respect to the dangerous relationship between bare feet and hookworm, it is nevertheless true that a good deal of tripe has been written on the matter. To say that these children can't afford shoes is true. It had better be added, though, that they would refuse to wear them if they could afford them: also, that summer shoes, in a warm country, are as useful as neckties for polar exploration: also that for growing children new shoes have to be bought each fall whether or not the old are worn out, because they are outgrown. Only two considerations make this subject serious at all: one, again, is the hookworm; the other is the fact that some children can't be afforded shoes for winter, go to school with their feet wrapped in sacks, or for that same reason stay at home.

Junior wears overalls every day of the week and Sunday, too, blue and store-bought. All summer his feet are a flycrawled, festered crust of sores: bites scratched and dewpoisoned, and swollen to their worst in dog days, and disinfected by coaloil and turpentine: the routine summer status of the feet for a country boy his age; the routine medicine for all minor injuries. (Perhaps it would be well to reconsider the shoe question; but bear in mind how normal and unnoticed this is.) Charles has some yellow, home-made overalls, but more of the time he wears a faded, twopiece blue-and-white suit caught together at the waist by four big buttons. Squeaky has a whole flock of dresses which no doubt come in handy for future babies (and no doubt have done so for Charles; some of them even for Junior). The best he has is a town-bought, very Nursery job with pink flowers and white rabbits printed on a blue ground, all laundered quite pale. The dressing of babies up to three or so is very simple, and is uncomplicated by genital genteelism. In hot weather they often go naked as jaybirds. The dresses are short and bell-shaped, usually split down the back with a single button at the nape. Babies let loose in such garments, especially those in the amphibious stage between crawling and walking, look comic and irrelevant in them, trailing them wide on the floor beside their shrimpish nudity, like dogs dressed up by children.

Most of Floyd's clothes are store-bought. Now and then a woman, and more frequently a maturing girl, buys a readymade dress. But most of the clothes are homemade on the sewing machine which next to the beds and stove is the least dispensable article of furniture. During the spring and summer some occasional scraping of money goes into bits of cloth—how little the money is, the preponderance of babies' dresses indicates—but the only real buying of clothes and cloths comes in the fall.

The other two families have been going longer

than the Burroughses: and pride over clothes and such breaks down with age. The Tingles could ill afford pride anyhow. The Fields and Tingles buy some clothes; but clothes are a foolish thing to spend on when cash is scarce and when flour and fertilizer sacks are plentiful. Fields has store overalls, and Sunday clothes (Tingle wears a new, tieless workshirt for Sunday), and his wife and Ruby and their children all have snatches and remnants of garments homemade of store cloth: but Mrs. Fields's town dress is plain as a nightgown, and as flimsy: basted together out of coarse pillowslip cotton; and for the rest, everything is fertilizer and floursacks, for her and her children, with the brands and insignia and poundage still smiling thru. Fields himself wears an extremely handsome fertilizer sack shirt. This handsomeness is only fair to mention: also, as a landowner would tell you, they cover their nekkidnuss all right: the other sides of the story are, we trust, self-evident. Fields also wears a work-hat, a torn, pierced, sewn-together, cockeyed, ex-best hat that any Dartmouth man of ten years back would forfeit at least the Freshman game with St. Anselm's prep for. The Fieldses make and wear these sackcloths frankly enough, and yet surreptitiously as compared with the Tingles. The Tingles for the most part have dropped entirely out of the realm of cotton prints, and have invested spaciously in very coarse, creamcolored cotton that was intended for sheeting. They mend and keep clothes even longer than the other two families; so they have quite a lot of them. Ida Ruth wears just a floursack, or a simple smock of sheetingcotton: and for Sundays and company, pink mercerized drawers. Sadie and Laura Minnie Lee have a choice of sheeting or guanosack dresses, totally plain, and sheeting overalls. They wear the overalls, usually, without shirts. The two boys have homemade overalls, guanosack shirts, and shallownapped corduroy pants which are far too worn to whistle as they walk. Flora Bee and Elizabeth have more variety, as befits young women. Flora Bee has her quota of sacks; her sheeting is trimmed, some of it, with pale pink gingham, and the collars are flounced; and besides that she has an old, fancy, ruined, curtain-lace blouse, with drabbled ribbons running in it, and a bright bold cotton print such as the town girls wear to the Post Office up in

Moundville. Work and weather and diet and the desperate knowledge that it is an attractive dress bar her from ever being mistaken for a girl to whom such clothes come natural: wearing it, she looks as though she has stolen it. Besides a number of plain sack and sheeting dresses, Elizabeth has a sheeting dress decorated with a half-cape of rough blue cotton, and, for best, a translucent, dead-black crepe sown with twinkling beads and sweated open alarmingly at the armpits. All among these girls, by the way, scatter a few strings of glass beads and a belt or so with a sporty buckle, to garnish and complete the picture.

Mrs. Tingle wears sacks and sheets all week and a dead-black dress, equally designless, on Sunday. She is barefoot, even on Sunday.

Some of these clothes are in fair shape: most of them are torn and sweated and befouled and patched and stitched far beyond any Bureau of Charities conception of what old-clothes means.

For work in the sun, most of the children and some of the women wear straw hats: modified, crackling sombreros. The Tingles alone among the three families go in for cornshuck hats, and they go in strong. A straw will cost anywhere from fifteen to fifty cents. In a day, one of the older girls can construct a hat out of cornshucks which will do just as well and which is, in fact, bright-fibered as platinum in the sun and thoroughly beautiful. Wearing one places you low in the social scale, though.

So much for the clothes.

CHAPTER 5

Work

Food: Clothing: Shelter.
The Lives of most men on the earth are spent in
getting these things.

F ew tenants have any strong or hopeful interest in the cotton they raise: they raise it because that is what they were rented their land and their home for. The greatest good it can do them is small against the work they have put into it. What they care more about is the corn they raise and the peas, the produce of the garden, and such little strips of sorghum, yams, peanuts, as they may (or may not) be permitted to plant: for these mean not doubtful cash and possible debt and another's profit in which they can have no heart, but life itself. We shall detail none of the task and process of raising these crops. Raising cotton is

PREVIOUS SPREAD: COTTON FIELD

what they are there for, what they must pour most of their lives into, and why they are alive at all. We shall not exhaustively detail that work either, for you can find it well covered many times elsewhere. But you should realize that it is at the dead center of their existence. They lean the weight of their lives on one end of a crowbar, that lifts such life as they have on its far end: and cotton and hard land is the crude bight. So here is a short account of the job it is for a tenant to raise cotton.

In the late fall or middle February he takes down the brittle forest of last year's crop with clubs or a cutter. In fulfillment of an obligation to his landlord he borrows a second mule and with a two-horse plow, runs up the levees, that is the terraces. Then the actual work begins, with what is planted where and with what grade and amount of fertilizer determined by the landlord, who will also criticize, advise, and govern his methods of cultivation. But this is the tenant's job, on which he has spent ten or forty years: back to the tenant.

He takes a twister, which is about the same as a turning plow, and, heading the mule concentrically, broadcasts; breaks the land broadcast; laying open as broad and deep a ribbon of stiff earth as the mules' strength and his own strength of guidance can manage: eight wide by six deep with a single-horse plow, twice that with a double, is good.

If you have two mules or like Fields and Tingle can double up, it is best to broadcast. (Then you lay out the furrows three and a half foot apart with a shovel plow; put down fertilizer; then by four furrows with a turning, plow, twist the land back over the fertilized furrow.) But if you have only one mule you break what you have time to and for the rest, bed, that is, start the land. There are two beddings. The first is hardbedding: breaking the hard pan between the rows.

Set the plow parallel of the line of stalks and to their right: follow each row to its end and up the far side: the dirt lays open always to the right. Then set the plow close in against the stalks and go around again. The stalk-stubble is cleaned out this second time round and between each two rows is a bed of soft dirt. That is the first bedding.

Then drop guano along where the stalks were, by machine or by horn. Most tenants buy a horn, or make it as Fields has done. It is a long tin cone, small end low, with a wood handle. Hold it in the left hand; take the guano in rhythmic fistfuls from the incipient frock slung heavily at your right side. After you have strowed the gyewanner you turn the dirt back over with two plowings just as before: and that is the second bedding. Pitch the bed shallow, or you won't be able to work it right.

If you have done all this right you haven't got a blemish in all your land that is not broke: and you are ready to plant.

There are three harrs you might use but the springtoothed harrow is best. The longtoothed section harrow tears your bed to pieces; the shorttoothed section is better but catches on snags and is more likely to pack your bed than loosen it. The springtooth moves lightly but incisively with a sort of knee-action to the modulations of the ground, and it jumps snags. You harr just one row at a time and right behind the harr comes the planter. It is rather like a tennis court marker. A little plow slivers open the dirt; just at its heel the seed runs out in a spindling stream; a flat wheel flats the dirt over: a light, tender, iron sexual act entirely worthy of settling beside the die-log, and the sweep of the broadhanded arm.

Depending on the moisture and the soil it will be five days to two weeks before the cotton will show. Cultivating begins as soon as it shows an inch.

The first job is barring off. Set a five to six inch twister, the smallest you have, close in to the stalks as possible, as close as the breadth of a finger if you are good at it, and throw the dirt to the middle. Alongside your plow is a wide tin defender, which doesn't allow a blemish to fall on the young plants.

Then comes the first of the four sweepings. The sweeps are blunt stocks shaped like stingrays. Over their blunt foreheads and broad shoulders they neither twist nor roll but shake the dirt from the middle to the beds on either side. For the first sweeping you still use the defender, and you use a little stock but the biggest you dare to; probably the eighteen inch.

Next comes the chopping, with which the whole family down through children of eight of seven helps, or rather, works all day. Chopping is a simple hard and hot job. It is simply thinning the cotton to a stand, hills a foot to sixteen inches apart, two to four stalks to the hill; done with an eight- to ten-inch hoeblade. You cut the cotton flush to the ground, with a semi-blow of the blade that aches first the forearms and in time the whole spine.

Then comes the second sweeping, with the twenty to twenty-two-inch stock you will use from then on: then comes hoeing, another job for the whole family; then you run the middles, that is, put down soda by hand or horn or machine. (Soda makes the weed; guano puts on the fruit.) Then comes the third sweeping: and then another hoeing. The first and second sweepings you have gone pretty deep. The stuff is small and you want to give loose ground to your feed roots. The third is shallow: the feed roots have extended within danger of injury.

The fourth sweeping is so light a scraping that it is scarcely more than a ritual, like a barber's last delicate moments with his own soul before he holds the mirror up to the dark side of your skull. The cotton has to be treated very carefully. By this last sweeping it is making. Break roots, or lack rain, and it is stopped dead as a hammer. (The language of tenants, among other nonliterary and scarcely literate people, is full of surrealism of that quality.)

This fourth sweeping is the operation more properly known as laying by. From now on to picking time, everything is up to the sky, the dirt, and the cotton itself. It is from now, in mid July, for five or six weeks on, that you have nothing to do and no rations money. You look for work and by great luck get some, or you look until you are sickened with looking, and sit down to take your leisure. Mile on mile on mile on mile, driving in midsummer, on the porch of nineteen shacks in twenty you see the same sight, formal as a dream: the whole family, blank in the eyes as fish, sitting in stiff rows, speechless in their chairs, like the wives in Bluebeard's basement, slack as meats on butchers' hooks, more dead than death: the adolescent daughters in their cleanest happiest prints. What this is like extended, like a lack of breath in too-deep water, through four months of the wetness and cold and knee-deep mud of the winter: what it does to the heart and brain of its victims: would be a pleasure to make unbearably clear. It is happening now. But only being there could make it clear: a tenant who is otherwise articulate shuts up as if he were shy of it. The trouble is, the public schools have not trained him in the ability to talk about abstractions, and food, and the uses of a useless day, and existence itself, are all very close to being abstractions in the winter.

But it is midsummer. Here is what the cotton is doing with its time. Each square points up: that is to say, on twig-ends, certain of its fringed leaves point themselves into the form of an infant prepuce: each square points up; and opens a white flat flower which turns pink the next day, purple the next, shrivels, and falls, the next: its fall forced upon it by the growth, at the base of the bloom, of the boll. Developments from square to bloom consume three weeks in the early summer, ten days in the later, longer heat. The blooming keeps on all summer. The development of the boll from the size of a pea to that point when, at the size of a big walnut, it darkens and dries and its white contents explode it, takes five to eight weeks.

Meantime there are enemies. Bitterweed, rag-weed, Johnsongrass; the weevil, the army worm; the slippery chances of the sky. Bitterweed is easily extinguished and won't come back up again. Ragweed will, with another prong every time. That weed can suck your crop to death. Johnsongrass, it takes hell and scissors to control. You can't control it in the drill (the row) with your plowing. If you just cut it off with the hoe, it is high as your thumb by the next morning. The best you can do is dig up the root with the corner of your hoe, and that doesn't hold it back any too well.

The weevil is much less dangerous an enemy than he used to be. Army worms are devils. The biggest of them are the size of your little finger. They eat leaves and squares and young bolls. You get a light crop of them at first. They web up in the leaves and become flies; the flies lay eggs; the eggs become army worms by the million and you can hear the rustling of their eating like a brushfire. They are a menace but they are easier to control than the weevil. You mix arsenic poison with a sorry grade of flour and dust the plants late of an evening (afternoon) or soon of a morning (premorning): the dew makes a paste of it that won't blow off.

It's a very unusual year when you do well with both your most important crops, because they need rain and sun in such disparate amounts. Cotton needs much less rain than corn: it is really a sun flower. *If* it is going to get a superflux of rain, that will best come before the cotton is blooming. And if it must rain during that part of the summer when a fairsized field is blooming a bale a day, it had best rain late in the evening when the blooms are shutting, not in the morning and midday. For then the bloom is blared out flat; rain easily gets in it and hangs on it; it shuts wet, sours, and sticks to the boll; next morning it turns red and falls. Often the boll comes off with it. But the boll that stays on is sour and rotted and good for nothing. It isn't therefore at all surprising that the religious faith of tenants is clearest and deepest in their prayers for a good season (a good rain) or for sunlight: weather is the least controllable essential in their uncontrollable lives. Nor is it in the least surprising that not one of those miraculous demonstrations of the sky which compose an Alabama year arouses in them the lightest reflex toward what is known as beauty. The weather is as organic to them as their own livers, and just as important and just as customary.*

*They have in fact the stormfear that many primitive peoples share: and wind is terrifying to them as cloud and lightning and thunder. You can never tell what's in a cloud, Burroughs says. Arn, and dogs, draws lightning, he adds. Families, when the man is away, hurry to join each other beneath the blackening of the air. They draw together in shuttered and latched rooms; the children are silent; Mrs. Burroughs sits with her hand on her knees and her palms to her ears. The men are responsibly brave for the sake of their families, but are not in the least ashamed of the fact of their own fear.

CHAPTER 6

Picking Season

L ate in August the fields begin to whiten more rarely with late blooms and more frequently with cotton and then still thicker with cotton, like a sparkling ground starlight; and the wide tremendous light holds the earth beneath a glass vacuum and a burning glass. The bolls are rusty green, are bronze, are split and burst and splayed open in a loose vomit of cotton. The split bolls are now *burrs*, hard and edged as chiseled wood, pointed as thorns, three-, four-, and five-celled. There is a great deal of beauty about a single burr and the cotton slobbering from it and about a whole field opening. The children and once in a while a very young or a very old man, are excited and eager to start picking. It is a joy that scarcely touches most men and any women, though, and it wears off in half a morning and is gone for a year.

Picking is simple and terrible work. Skill will

help you; endurance will come in handy; but neither makes it a bit easier. Over your right shoulder you have slung a long sack that trails to the ground. You work with both hands as fast and steadily as you can. The trick is to get the cotton between your fingertips at its very roots on the burr in all three or four or five gores at once so that it brings out clean at one pluck: an easy job with one burr in ten, where the cotton is ready to fall; with the rest, the fibers are tight and tricky. The other trick is against this thoroughness and obligation of maximum speed, not to hurt your fingers on the burrs any worse than you can help. You would have to try hard, to break your flesh on any burr: a single raindrop is only scarcely instrumental in ironing a mountain flat. An hour's picking, your hands are just limbered up. A week, and you are favoring your fingers. The later of the three to five times over the field, the last long weeks of the season, you might be happy to swap them for boils.

Meantime, too, you are working in sunlight that stands on you with the serene weight of deep seawater, and in heat that makes your jointed and muscled and finestructured body flow like one indiscriminate oil, and the brilliant weight of heat is piled upon you heavier and heavier all the time and the eyes are masked in stinging sweat and the head perhaps is gently roaring like a private blowtorch, and less gently pulsing with ache. Also the bag, that can hold a hundred pounds, is filling as you drag it from plant to plant, four to nine burrs to a plant to be rifled swiftly, then the load shrugged along another foot or two and the white row stretched ahead to a blur and innumerably multiplied by other white rows, and bolls in the cleaned row behind you already like slow popcorn in the heat and the sack still heavier and heavier, so that it pulls you back as a beast might rather than a mere dead weight.

Also, cotton plants are low, so that in this heat and immanent weight of light and the heavying sack you are dragging, you are continuously stooped over even if you are a child, and bent very deep if you are a man or a woman. A strong back is a big help but not even the strongest back was built for that treatment, and there combine not just at the kidneys, and rill down the thighs and up the spine and athwart the shoulders, the ticklish weakness of gruel or water, and an aching that increases in geometric progression, and at length, in the small of the spine, a literal sensation of yielding, buckling, splintering, and breakage: and all of this, even though the mercy of nature has strengthened and hardened your flesh and anaesthetized your nerves and your powers of reflection and imagination, reaches in time the brain and the more mirrorlike nerves, and thereby makes itself much worse than before.

Later in the season you are relieved of the worst of the heat. In time, you exchange it for a coolness which many pickers like even less because it slows and chills the lubricant garment of sweat they work in, and seriously slows and stiffens the by then painfully sore fingers.

The idiom has been overused but it is accurate: picking goes on each day from can't to can't: sometimes, if there's a rush, the Tingles continue by moonlight. In the blasting heat of the first of the season unless there is a rush—to beat a rain, to make up a wagonload—it is customary to quit work an hour and a half and even two hours in the worst part of the day and sit or lie in the shade and possible draft of the

hallway asleep or half-asleep after dinner. This time off narrows as the weeks go by and a sense of rush and the wish to be done with it grow on the pickers and come through from the landlord. There are tenants who have no midday meal. Those we are speaking of have it. It is of course no parallel in heartiness and variety to the proud enormous dinners cooked up for harvest hands in the wheat country and accounted and painted with Zest, Gusto, and even Zowie by certain lovers of what they call the American Scene. It is the same everyday food, with perhaps a little less variety than in midsummer, hastily cooked by a woman who has hurried in exhausted from the fields a couple of jumps ahead of her family, and served in the dishes she rushily rinsed before she hurried out a couple of jumps behind them.

There has been a certain exaggeration about child labor in the cotton fields: essentially none, but stupid a little, and worth a word or two. The exaggerations have chalked up child labor as a crime a hundred per cent against the landlord or his overseers. They—particularly the overseer—have some direct and a strong indirect part in it. But two facts the correspondents have overlooked. One is that it is customary as breathing on all farms, even the Jersiest and most Kulak you can imagine, for the children of the family to help with the work. That is part of the whole structure of any family that lives directly off the land. The other fact is that Southern farmers more strongly than others retain still the delineaments of the primitive family anywhere: a patri- or matriarchy (in the South it is patriarchal; in the American middle class it is matriarchal and on an uglier plane)—a patriarchy into which children are born unquestioning slaves until by their own physical or mental strength they free themselves.* Still another fact that has nothing to do with the tenant system is that cotton requires more labor than most other crops and that the labor of your children is free. The economic skeleton of these three facts is plain as the skull on your throat and so solidly sustains the arguments of those who ignore it that it is odd indeed that they do ignore it.

*Deeper in the Southern mountains these lines are proportionally more sternly drawn. Southerners of twenty years back can remember vividly how, along the millhouse streets, deep country couples who had raised a brood to working age and brought them to market sat on their sterns on porch after porch while their children, at the spindles, brought in the bacon or, rather, sowbelly.

However, there is certainly a line. Cross it, and the work children do most certainly becomes child labor. Every tenant family crosses it and the fact that few are aware of crossing it is irrelevant. In that country you speak of a family not as a family but as a force: and with good reason. Nothing brilliant is expected of a four-year-old but he will do a fair amount of picking along with the others; you cannot learn him too young. By the time he is seven he is no longer able to think of it, ever, as play. By the time he is twelve he has long outgrown any sense of privilege, pride, or novelty in plowing, too: and by that time if not before it is likely to seem logical as well as necessary that he quit school. All of the same goes for a girl. The baby meanwhile is lying in the field or rolling around in the white load of the woven-oak basket. A little older, say two, and he is picking his hat or his skirt full. There are sometimes shifts into gayety in the picking, or excitement—a race between the two children, a snake killed—but mostly it is silent, serious, and lonely work.

Floyd Burroughs is a very poor picker. When he was a child he fell in the fireplace and burnt the

flesh off the flat of both hands, so his fingers are stiff and slow and the best he has ever done in a day is 150 pounds. Average for a man is nearer 250. His back hurts him badly, too, so he usually picks on his knees, the way other pickers rest; and a man walking on his knees down a white shudder of heat is something for painters of peasants to look into. Allie Mae picks about the average for a woman—150 to 200 pounds a day. She is fast with her fingers until the work exhausts her. Lucile picks 150 pounds a day. Junior hasn't yet got into his stride. Fields has been slowed down by poor health for several years now. His wife is strong and competent and her mother is still a good picker (and a vindictive hand with an axe) so in spite of having only one child old enough to be any use they can get in the crop without hiring a hand. The Tingle boys are all right when their papa is on hand to make them work: otherwise they are likely just to clown, and tease their sisters. Sadie is very quick. Summer before last, when she was just eight, she picked 110 pounds in the day in a race with Laura Minnie Lee. Last summer she was slowed up by runarounds that were losing her two nails (caused by the diet plus

PREVIOUS SPREAD: TINGLE DRIVING COTTON TO THE GIN

dirt and not much fun among the burrs) but she was picking steadily. Mrs. Tingle used to pick 300 and 350 pounds a day but sickness has slowed her to less than 200 now. It is possible that Mrs. Tingle is something of a fantast, though, and indeed in all the above we must bear in mind the possibilities of Homeric brag: according to general publicity surrounding the Rust machine, 100 pounds a day is good picking.

Commonly, cotton is stored in a small structure in the field, the cotton house. None of these three families has one. The Burroughses store in one of their outbuildings; the Fieldses on their front porch, raising planks around it; the Tingles in their spare room. Children enjoy playing in it, tumbling, jumping, diving, burying each other; sometimes they sleep in it, as a sort of treat. Rats like it, too, to make nests in, and that draws ratsnakes. When the home scales have weighed out fourteen hundred pounds of cotton it is loaded on the high-boarded wagon and taken to gin. A man is "free" to take his cotton to whatever gin he pleases but that means generally the gin his landlord owns or has an interest in. The same goes for what store you trade at. Over and over again you hear tenants say, innocently enough, too, that there's never no use gitting a man agin ya.

The children take turns riding in, bale by bale and year by year: they are likely to be cleaned up as for Saturday afternoon, and they are happy and excited. And there is for that matter a happiness and excitement, and a raw, festal quality about it, this one of the tremendous slow parade of muledrawn, crawling wagons, creaking under the year's blood-sweated and prayed-over work, on all roads drawn in, from the slender red roads of all the South and onto the Southern highways, a wagon every few hundred yards, crested now with a white and now with a black family, all towards these little trembling lodes that are the gins, and all and in each private heart towards that climax of one more year's work which yields so little at best, and nothing so often, and worse to so many hundreds of thousands.

The gin, too, the wagons in line, the people waiting on the wagons, the suspended whiteshirted men on the platform, the emblematic sweep of the great-shouldered iron beam scales cradling gently in the dark doorway, the insignia of justice, the landlords in their shirtsleeves at the gin or relaxed in swivels beside the painted safes in their little offices, the heavy-muscled young men in baseball caps who tumble the bales with sharp short hooks, the leafers drawn there to have their batteries recharged with the vicarious violence that is in process in the bare and weedy outskirts of the bare and brutal town—all that also in its hard, slack, sullen way, is dancelike and triumphal. The big blank surfaces of ribbed tin, bright and sick as gas in the sunlight, square their darkness round a shuddering racket that is mystery to these we speak of. All it means to a tenant is this: he gets his ticket and his bale number; waits his turn in line; drives under as they hise the ginhead; they let him down the suction pipe; he cradles its voracity down through the crest of and round and round his stack of cotton till the last lint has leapt up from the wagonbed. Wandering loose out back, his son may happen upon the tin and ghostly interior of the seed shed, against whose roof and rafters a pipe extends a steady sleet of seed and upon all whose interior surfaces and all the air, a dry nightmare fleece trembles like the fake snows of Christmas movies. Out in front he can see the last of the cotton snowlike relaxing in pulses down a space of dark into the compress. The bale is lifted like a Roxy organ, the presses unlatched, numbered brass tag attached, the ties fastened: it hangs in the light breathing of the scales. A little is slivered from it; the staple length is taken. (Of the type raised in this vicinity it is ⅞ths-inch to an inch.) The ginning charge per scale varies a little; hangs around $4. On anything exceeding 550 pounds there is an extra charge of a cent a pound; for this overweight strains the press. There are plenty of buyers on hand, ranging between Vergil Davis who clerks in the town's biggest general store (the Moundville Mercantile, popularly known as Davis's) through legmen for Southern mills. A half-cropper has little to say about the sales; a renter a fair amount. The cotton may be sold right off the platform; and may wait on, for better prices, late into December. If it waits it may be stored in the Government warehouse; it may be left outdoors. Alone among Moundville landlords the Tidmore brothers have a warehouse of their own, and they charge their tenants no storage. The tenant gets nothing on his cotton until settling-up time, at the end of the season; the landlord's first

cotton-money by invariable custom pays off his fertilizer bill. What the tenant does get bale by bale is the
money on his share of the cottonseed, on which his
living depends. A landlord sometimes makes a joking
feint of withholding that money against outstanding
debts and, somewhat less often, carries out the joke.
But generally the tenant's business of that day ends
as he leaves his landlord with six dollars or so in his
pocket. The exodus from town is even more formal
than the parade in was. It has taken almost exactly
eighteen minutes to gin each bale (once the waiting
was over), and each tenant has done almost exactly
the same amount of business afterward; and the tenants' empty, light-grinding wagons are distributed
along the roads in a likewise exact conjunction of
time and space apart: the time consumed by ginning
plus business; the space apart which, in that time, any
mule traverses at his classic somnambulist pace. It is
as if the people drawn in full and sucked dry were re-
stored, sown at large upon the breadth of their country, precisely as by some impersonal mechanic hand.

That happens as many times as you have picked
a bale; the field is gone over three to five times; the

height of the ginning season, when wagons are on the road before the least crack of daylight and the gin is still racketing after dark, in early October. After this comes hogkilling; and the milling of the corn and sorghum you have planted to come ready late; and specific consideration of whether or not to move to another man; the sky descends; the air becomes like dark glass; the ground hardens; the clay honeycombs with frost; the odors of pork and woodsmoke sharpen all over the country; and winter is on.

CHAPTER 7

Education

In spite of much that could be ventured to the contrary it would seem overwhelmingly certain that any fulness of the good which human existence is capable of must come in a clarity and health of brain and of feeling, of self-knowledge and of knowledge of the world, as well as in any clarity of physical action: and could be arrived at only through education or self-education, using those words in senses much broader than their common ones. It is not for us to invent a system of education which would have any relevance to what we are talking about: we wish merely to point out a few facts. One is that the intellect and the emotions are quite irrelevant to lives such as our three families are leading; so that education is likewise irrelevant to their lives. Another is that such education as they are exposed to is capable of doing them more harm than good. Another is that they are peculiarly ill-equipped for self-education. Still another is obvious: the damages of circumstance are peculiar by no means to the cotton tenant or, indeed, to any single class such as the working class: the thriving business done by bughouses highpriced enough to get by as sanitariums is one proof of that which is superfluous to anyone interested to look about him, and into himself. Still another is likewise obvious: if by education can be meant not mere schooling in facts but a profound clearing and cleaning of the mental air, a real qualifying of a human being for existence, then education is all but nonexistent, and what passes for it is merely a more or less organized dispensary of poisons which may or may not take.

We are not therefore leveling any special attack against the Alabama school system, which to all intents and purposes is neither better nor worse than any other. Like others it fails to come within miles of essentials; like others it is almost inspiredly unintuitive and ineffectual in teaching even what it purports to teach. A few notes can suffice us, and will indicate plenty.

CROSSROADS STORE

School runs from middle September to the first of May. Country schoolchildren, with their lunches, are picked up by buses at seven-thirty in the morning, dropped again towards the early winter dark. The children of the families we speak of—it is the same of most children living off the highways—have a walk anyhow. In dry weather the bus gets up the side road as far as Tom Elliott's house. (Tom Elliot is a white-skinned, red-haired, ill-witted Negro who has nothing to do with our story.) The Tingle children walk half a mile to meet it. The Burroughs three-quarters. In wet weather the bus can't leave the highway; the Tingles walk two miles, the Burroughs a mile and a half (and back in the afternoon) in sometimes knee-deep clay.

There was talk last summer of graveling the road up further; though most of the fathers of families were beyond road age (forty-five). They can ill afford to do such work for nothing, though, and they and their Negro neighbors are in no position to pay taxes. Nothing had come of it within three weeks of the start of school; and probably nothing has.

Southern winters are wet, but the children keep

pretty well: Junior was absent only sixty-five and Lucile only fifty-three days out of a possible 150-odd, and they were unexcused only eleven and nine times respectively. Twenty-three of Junior's and a proportionate number of Lucile's absences fell in the last two months, which are dedicated to work as well as wetness. Needed at home, Lucile missed several schooldays late in her second year, including the final examinations. Her marks had been good but no chance was given her to make up the examination and she had to take the year straight over: reasonably criminal treatment of an intelligent child but not peculiar to Alabama and perhaps made up for in Junior's case. He is now in the second grade for the second year. He is there at all thanks to the law which automatically passes a pupil after three years in a grade. It is true of public schools that bright pupils are held back by the others. It is true also that slow pupils are smothered beneath the others beyond any hope of the sort of help they need.

The school itself is a windowy, healthful, brick structure in Moundville which perfectly exemplifies the American genius, so well shown forth in "low-cost" housing, for sterility, dullness, and general gutlessness in seizing any opportunity for reform or improvement. It is the sort of building a town such as Moundville is proud of, and a brief explanation of the existence of such a building in such a country will be worthwhile. Of late years Alabama has Come Awake to Education. Its counties have received appropriations in proportion to the size of their school population. The school population of Hale County is five black to one white, and since not a cent has gone into Negro schools, such neat buildings as this are possible: for white children. Negroes still sardine themselves, 100 and 120 strong, into stoveheated oneroom shacks which would reasonably house a fifth of them if the walls, roof, and windows were tight. But then as one landlord said and as many more would agree: "I don't object to Nigrah education, up through fourth or fift grade maybe, but not furden nat: I believe too strongly in white supremacy."

The bus service and the building the white children are schooled in, even counting the muddy walk, are downright effete, of course, compared to what their parents had. The schooling itself is a different matter, too: much more Modern. The boys and girls alike are exposed to Art and to Music; and the girls learn the first elements of tapdancing. The art of course has nothing to do with art, if the children's favorite drawings are any indication: nor has the music anything to do with music, unless the piping of Cute children's songs composed by dehydrated spinsters and child psychologists be taken as such. Moreover, though the sight of a gawkily graceful sharecropper's daughter clogging out abysmal barefoot imitations of Eleanor Powell is a pleasure, of some odd sort, it is not an unmingled pleasure. Not that any vote for fingerpainting, rhythms, and morris-dancing is in order. We mean only to observe that the problem of esthetic eye-opening and training has reached no solution, either rarefied or practical, in Moundville's public school.

Textbooks are so cheap almost anyone can afford them; though it must be added that Floyd, a couple of years back, had to sell a hog, badly needed for winter meat, to afford them. A few titles and a few quotations, thought over just a little, will suggest to you how much more thoughtful of The Child

Mind textbook writing, and teaching, is today than yesterday; will suggest also just how effectual chance is. Let us also remember, while we are about it, that few tenant children get beyond grade school, and that even here we shall imply the far reaches of the book-knowledge of the average. Here are some that were kicking round the Burroughs house last summer:

The Open Door Language Series—First Book: Language Stories and Games.

Trips to Take. Among the contents are poems by Vachel Lindsay, Elizabeth Madox Roberts, Robert Louis Stevenson, et cetera. Likewise a story titled: "Brother [sic] Rabbit's Cool Air Swing"; and subheaded: Old Southern Tale.

Outdoor Visits: Book Two of Nature and Science Readers. (Book One is Hunting.) Book two opens: "Dear Boys and Girls: in this book you will read how Nan and Don visited animals and plants that live outdoors."

Real Life Readers—New Stories and Old. A Third Reader. (With color photographs about as real-life as color photographs get.)

The Trabue-Stevens Speller. Just another speller.

Champion Arithmetic. Five hundred and ten pages: a champion psychological inducement to an interest in numbers. Final problem: Janet brought 1 ¼ lb. of salted peanuts and ½ lb. of salted almonds. Altogether she bought ___ lb. of nuts.

Floyd Burroughs can spell, read, and write his own name: beyond that he mires up. He got as far as the second grade. By that time there was work for him and he was slowminded anyway. Allie Mae can read, write, spell, and handle simple arithmetic: and even at this late date grasps and is excited by such matters as the simpler facts of astronomy and geology. Bud Fields quit school at twelve when he ran away and went to work in the mines. He can read,

write, and figure. So can his wife. Frank Tingle got as far as the fifth grade. He was bright, too. When his teacher said the earth turned on an axle he asked her was the axle set in posts, then. She said yes, she reckoned so. He said well, wasn't hell supposed to be under the earth and if so wouldn't they be all the time trying to chop the axlepost out from under the earth? But here the earth still was so what was all this talk about axles. Teacher never did bring up nothing about no axles after that. No sir, she never did bring up nothing about no durn axles after that. No sirree, she shore never did bring brang up nuthn about no blamed axles attah dayat. Tingle reads a little less like a child than the others and is rather smug about it: "I was readn whahl back na Progressive Farmer rr." Mrs. Tingle can neither read nor write. She went to school one day in her life and her mother got sick and she never went back.

Elizabeth quit school when she was in the fifth grade because her eyes hurt her bad ever time she studied books. There was no thought of glasses: if there had been they would have come from the five-and-ten like those her father wears, purely decoratively,

PREVIOUS SPREAD: GENERAL STORE, INTERIOR

of a Sunday. She has forgotten a good deal how to read. Flora Bee quit when Elizabeth did because she was lonesome. She still reads and quite possibly will not forget how. Newton and William are in the fourth grade. In another year or two they will be big enough for full farm work and they will be needed for it. Laura Minnie Lee and Sadie are in the second grade. Sadie, though she is so shy she has to write out her reading lessons, is brighter than average; and Laura Minnie Lee, her mother says, is brighter than Sadie, reads and writes smoothly, and "specially delights in music." Ida Ruth is too young for school.

The Tingles are known of and listed as "problem" children: their attendance record is extremely bad; their conduct is not good. Besides their four-mile walk in bad weather here is some more explanation. They have to wear clothes and shoes which make them the obvious butts for the better-heeled brats in town. Among the poorest even of poor whites, they are looked down on even by most levels of the tenant farmer class. They are uncommonly sensitive and easily hurt, and their loneliness is of a sort to inspire savage loyalty among them. They are Problems all right; and the problem won't be simplified as these wild and oversexed children grow into adolescence. The girls in particular seem inevitably marked out for incredible cruelty and mistreatment.

Ruby Fields may have started to school this fall: probably not, for it was to depend on whether the road was graveled so she would not have the long walk to the bus alone or with the Tingle children. She has a bloodlipped, weasel-like intelligence that might or might not find engagement in the squarehead cogs of public schooling.

Junior Burroughs is probably hopeless so far as schooling is concerned. Perhaps he has inherited his father's slowmindedness and perhaps, also, his father's disease, of which more in its place. Lucile likes school, especially all about the history of our country. We have already remarked on her parents' intention to send her on through school, and on her desire to become a teacher. In view of what education is, it is perhaps needless to point out that should she become a teacher, that would hardly be a change for the better.

CHAPTER 8

Leisure

P ossibly the most important thing to a human being, once he is alive and possessed of the means
of sustaining life, is that he should do the work
he cares most to do and is best capable of doing. If
there is anything else of quite such importance to
him (always barring the Higher Affections) it would
fall under the head of Leisure, and how best to use
and enjoy it. Every detail of circumstance and nearly
every detail of so-called education reduces freedom
in choice of occupation to an all but nonexistent mar-
gin, for people such as the Burroughses. Thanks to the
same circumstances and education they have about
the least chance imaginable of so much as dreaming
what work they would be capable of, and would best
like to do, if any breadth of choice were possible. It is
therefore comfortable to realize that they have, anyhow, a great deal of leisure. Six months of the year

there is little farm work to do; every Saturday, except in a rush, work stops at noon and everyone goes to Moundville; Sunday is always a day of rest, and often even during work time, as we have seen, there are eases in the day.

But when we say leisure we are thinking of all social relations, and of the enjoyment of life. We would be the first to admit that taking America by and large the leisure of its people is if anything more grim than the work, but our subject here is the leisure of the tenant farmer: a subject difficult to write of journalistically, since it is so nearly an abstraction.

There are virtually none of the narcotics to which almost any more prosperous class is addicted. There are very, very few newspapers or magazines. What there are, are saved. The covers and pretty pictures are pasted on the walls; the children save and look at the comic sections over and over. Frank Tingle alone among them enjoys reading. He reads pulps, when he gets them, from kiver to kiver, and he sometimes reads a copy of the Progressive Farmer. Some years back, Floyd bought a fifty dollar Grafanola on the installment plan. (Judging by the music played at five-and-ten counters in the county seats, the white preference is for sweet as against hot, disliked as nigger music, and still more for whines like Lonely Days in Texas.) There are no radios. There are few cars, and they are invariably Model-Ts. None of them has the famous rustic pleasure of hewing closely to the Party Line. The infiltration of all that has to do with the outside world is slow, verbal, and distorted in transit.

Perhaps we may as well mention here what we lately referred to as the Higher Affections. It is almost but not quite safe to say that there is no such thing in that vicinity except, occasionally, in the phases of courtship and the early phases of marriage. We must make these qualifications. The Tingles, much more cut off from people than the others (by their "lowness" in the scale) appear to have an actual and active, mutual and fully distributed affection at least and sometimes love for each other. Fields and his wife, though he refers to her in her presence as this-woman-here, show signs of really enjoying each other. Mrs. Burroughs is very fond of her father and of her sister Mary, proud and fond of her daughter, and devoted to her youngest child as if he were the only thing that kept her alive, which perhaps he is. Floyd is fond and proud of his eldest son. But lovelessness is nevertheless overwhelmingly the impression you would get, and your impression would be confirmed in detail in the course of time. You can find the same, you may say, almost anywhere you look. We say only that the chances for good are at their slenderest in contexts such as we are here speaking of.

Friend is a word you will hear seldom, too. People don't have friends: they have kinfolks, and neighbors, and former neighbors, and acquaintances, many of whom they would without reflection make great efforts and sacrifices for; they get along with them more or less amiably.

The habitual expression of face and of gesture is serious, slow, and somewhat sad.

Children play routine games of marbles, crack-the-whip, hide-and-seek. There are also spontaneous games with dogs. A solitary such as Charles makes up gibberish by the hour that shows an idiot genius for rhythmic variety. Older children begin to show the painful restiveness of a maturing mind that has nothing to mature on, and of a sexual hunger that has no way to feed itself. The leisures of adolescence are particularly disturbing to watch; and their power alone to bore to frenzy would explain early marriages if nothing else did.

The social relations among the three families are limited. During easy parts of weekdays Mrs. Fields, with her children in tow, may visit Mrs. Burroughs, or vice versa, and they sit on the porch and drawl at each other. When the men are at work away from home, or looking for work, they have a somewhat richer social exchange than this: more people are seen in more variety; there is a loosening of tongues under the sunlight and searching, and in the reflection of a morning's events during a lunch period. At home, most of the family talk is during meals. There is just the hard substance of the day and direct future in it. Junior went out to the cotton house and there was a ratsnake jist a-dabbin at him, or, that black kitten went and had fits and he died ... The children, especially the little girls, sometimes spend overnight together: and the presence of a guest cheers everyone a good deal, though usually the pleasure is scarcely articulate. Very occasionally whole families will visit each other overnight. There was a good time two years ago the Burroughses still like to remember, when Bud was still living over in the swamp and his daughter Mary was home (one of the two times she has left her husband for good). They all went over and all of them but Allie Mae and Lily got drunk. Mary, she was just sloppy-drunk, she was so drunk she didn't know she was in the world. That same sort of party mixed with nonrelatives and with a fiddle and dancing added, is called a frolic. Frolics are not frequent among the white people, even when a good many of them live near together, and out this lonesome road none of the families has been on one for years. Thanksgiving and Christmas and Fourth of July are always big times. Last Fourth of July all the white people out that road had a picnic, and it was a good time for everyone until Mr. Peoples's nineteen-year-old idiot epileptic son throwed a fit and spoiled the fun.

It must be remembered of course that the six months of nominal leisure are somewhat qualified: they offer the derelict leisure of unemployment.

The two big leisure days, dependably, each week,

SUNDAY SINGING

are Saturday and Sunday. On Saturday, everyone goes to Moundville.

Whether Moundville need be "described" is a problem. It is a town on the small side of small and the mean (not tough, just mean) side of mean. Such towns have been nailed into the reading lobe of the American brain perhaps beyond need of further hammering. Barring church, however, it offers the people we are speaking of their total experience of what social students like to call communal life: it is market place and metropolis to them and to miles of country side. Moreover, it is that swatch of civilization which people of that countryside directly support: for nearly everyone—that is, Everyone—in town owns at least a little piece of land, and most landowners have some business interest in Moundville. So perhaps a few notes are in order.

Population around 500. Autoplates bearing the legend: "Heart of the Cotton Belt." A quarter of a mile off a State Highway. Hard by the biggest Mounds in Alabama, within which are the bones of diminutive Mongolians 3,500 years dead, now being exhumed at bargain cost by the boys in CC Camp Baltsell. Served by the Southern Railway. Three big corrugated tin gins owned and operated by combines of landowners. Low tin shed: cotton warehouses. A planing mill run by Joseph Mills, who has been prematurely logging in the vicinity for the past fifteen years and for whom Floyd and Tingle work. Mrs. Wiggins's Hotel and Café. Out front, a Negress jouncing the Wiggin baby in an elastic swing or, of a Saturday afternoon, middle-class (but not quite Class) housewives in clean best ginghams, watching the crowd, commenting, pulling their dresses loose from their skins. Two drug stores, run by the town's two senior doctors, serving gigantic quantities of Coca Cola and selling sadistic pulps to the men, ovarian pulps to the women, and patent medicines to all comers. Three general stores owned by the landowners in combine, their wares general as only the wares of Southern country stores can be. A Yellow Front store, one of a chain, specializing in groceries. A hardware store. A filling station. (Others out at the highway.) A mule market. A biggish new clean brick church with saintless windows that resemble an amalgam of oysters in need of fresh air: a landowners' church: Methodis or Babtis, what difference does it make. The homes of landowners: squarebuilt, in fair trim, set in bushy lawns on which are wooden animals; graded down to muggy houses which, if women, would not have shaved their underarms. Nothing Greek-revival. A colossally filthy, or in fairer words perfectly ordinary, Niggertown.

Saturdays: On the depot platform and the porch of the refrigerator shed lounge two identical groups: town boys of fifteen to twenty in the light pants, light shirt, and eyeshade or new straw which make the uniform of their kind and class; twitching with curbed sexuality and a less curbed violence: tinder for every crime from the seduction of Negresses to lynching. In front of the hotel: the fat-sterned mamas of the hamlet, sweating their sour cosmetics into dough. At the curbs enjoying curb service, or coursing the two blocks of business street quietly, over and over, in daddy's chivrolet coach, daughters of the landed gentry, girls who can only be described as bitchy. In the stores or threading the walks: the landowners and merchants, shirtsleeved, hatted, sweating with extreme busyness or taking time off for a stroll and a dope. In vacant grounds behind the low buildings, crowded and silent, the empty wagons, the mules twitching their hides against the flies. In the stores and on the walks and all over the streets: the tremendous shy and nearly silent swarm of whites and of Negroes drawn in out of the slow and laborious depths of the country, along the withered vine of their red roadsteads and along the sedanswept blue slags of highway, on mule, on mule-drawn wagon, and by foot hanging together, each family, like filings delicately aligned by a hidden magnet, doing their scraps of trading, meeting acquaintances and relatives otherwise seldom seen and jawing a little, with no demonstration even of pleasure, far less of fake effusiveness; shy even here and even here a little stunned by the urbanity of it all: alien to it: not at all of it: looked down on, a little contemptuously, by it: threaded steadily by a man upon whose belt-sustained overdose of bowels perches, toylike yet businesslike, a pistol in a black holster.

Among all these are the Burroughses and the Fieldses and a quota and sometimes all of the Tingles: They have come in crowded in one wagon, usually Tingle's. They buy their lard and flour and light groceries and, if there is money left, some gingersnaps or some peanutshaped, bananaflavored candy for the children; or a couple of yards of printed cotton; or, very occasionally, the men will sneak into a blind tiger and buy half a pint of corn, which they drink swiftly in the blinding heat and under whose influence their conduct is unpredictable. (They have a sense of guilt about drinking and consequently a viciously kiddish sense of joy about it; though they drink far less badly than the acned young men on the depot platform.)

Once in a great while a movie is shown on Saturday, in the Moundville School. That is all that need be said, because few of the parents and none of the children we are speaking of have ever seen one. Of course to many tenants, near the next bigger size of town, movies are less unfamiliar. Their Saturday fare may as well be mentioned, then: A Western always; a serial imitative of the adventures of Tarzan; a short comedy or musical about middle-class city life or Times Square. Occasionally a problem drama about the difficulties of being rich and looking like Miriam Hopkins, or a comedy of manners with dialogue which is a bad imitation at fourth remove of the dialogue of Philip Barry.

Every so often, Gypsies come through. It causes a certain amount of interest out in the country because they are mistaken for Injuns.

Last summer a merry-go-round (pronounced with the accent on go) set up in the vacant lot next the combined mayor's office and jail: beautifully sculpted horses painted in delirious colors; good primitive oils concealing the core of machinery; a jim crow sign in gold letters on red; mechanized Wurlitzer horns gaily blowing tunes of fifteen years old. Burroughs and Tingle got drunk and took rides. (Many adult Negroes, perfectly sober, rode, too.) Maybe there will be another one next summer. There is one running all the time up in Tuscaloosa but that is so far off (twenty-five miles) that, for instance none of the Burroughs children had ever seen it until last summer.

Sunday is the day of rest. Children are welcome to play, and sometimes a man gets quietly drunk, but it is a day of rest. People go to church some, less regularly perhaps than you might think, and pay each other visits, kin-to-kin mostly. A chicken is killed, in honor. While the women are fixing it and getting dinner ready, the men sit on the porch and talk or

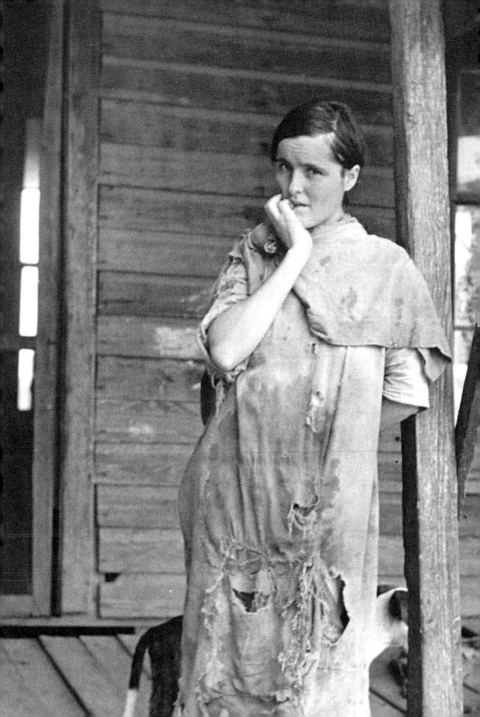

smoke or chew; the little girls retire into a lowvoiced and mysterious semi-privacy; the boys jab at the dirt with sticks or knives. While the men are eating dinner, the women wait on them and brush flies away. While the women and children are eating, the men sit and talk. Later they get up and go quietly around the fields, or examine a bee-gum, or lean over the rail of a hogpen. The women drift away in pairs, or with a child, into the woods, and come back quietly to sit on the porch and talk. When the men come back and take the chairs they go in and sit on the bed. There is no point in recording the talk. It is endless, unhurried, unembarrassed by silence, of neighbors, crops, stock, sickness, cooking, scandal, hunting, death, fortune, misfortune, types of fertilizer, a leaking roof, government jobs, the chance of a job, childbearing, the weather, all depending on the sex of the talkers and the length of distance and time they have been apart. There is very little communication between the women and the men.

Somewhat unusually isolated, these three families have less "company" than the average. Bud Fields sees his two sons fairly often; Burroughs, his mother and a sister in Moundville on Saturdays (she is married to Fields's son Edward); Tingle, less often, his brother, who lives four miles back of them out the road: but the radius is small, and seldom exceeded.

There aren't enough white people in the neighborhood to support a church, so these three families are deprived of what in another place would be the only full-blown social spiritual and esthetic event in their lives. The meetings in deep country go on for hours and intensify, during the dead weeks before picking, into revivals.

So they make it up the best way they can. Up till the year before last they held meetings in Tingle's home, in the spare room where he stores his cotton. Everyone looked forward to the meetings and everyone came, including a number of tough and scornful outsiders. As time wore on the meetings got too rough. Finally the Tidmores gave them permission to use an abandoned one-room nigger-shack a little piece down the road. For no reason that anyone understands, there has been no trouble since.

The meetings are held Wednesday and Friday

evenings except when work is at a rush, and every Sunday right after early dinner. No one specially regrets missing a weeknight meeting, but everyone looks forward to the Sundays except Fields, who is "not a religious man." None of them are especially religious for that matter, except over the weather and in fear of death, but they would all be deeply shocked if you expressed any doubt about the existence and nature of God; they care a great deal about the singing and, to a person who has nothing on earth and is done with hoping, it is an obvious and, when necessary, a profound and cathartic comfort to be sure that in the long run all is for the best and the poor man will be taken care of. They are of different sects but the depth of country and tradition makes them all much alike in action and tone. These meetings are non-sectarian, and it causes no one any apparent discomfort.

After a certain amount of preliminary singing, Tingle or a neighbor named Peoples asks each person present to quote a verse of the Bible. "The-*Lord*givethandtheLordhathtakenawayblessedbethe-nameofthe*Lord*." One child said "Let not your heart be troubled" (a favorite verse); the next said "Jesus wept": and well he might.

After that the leader reads a chapter from the New Testament and expounds it, verse by verse; and after that the singing resumes in good earnest, everyone crowded behind the torn forty-year-old hymnal. The hymns are of the Moody-Sankey tradition crossed with the subtler and more swinging intervals and rhythms of the Southern poor whites or mountaineers. They are sung with violence by the leaders; hummed or growled by the more shy. The leaders are Frank Tingle and his two eldest daughters. Tingle picked up sight-reading in one night at singing-school and has a somewhat fallible talent for harmony and improvisation. His voice is a loud bugling bay and it brackets the whole male register. His daughters, who have learned the tunes and most of the words by heart, strain and tighten their naturally pleasant voices continually, in hopeless competition with him. They are expert and responsible in starting off the new verse the instant the old one is done with. His two boys likewise break their unchanged throats. His two smaller girls sing slenderly like violins, and fall into silences of shyness over the sound of their own voices. All the hymns are long, five and six verses plus chorus; they all have a pitch and roll to them; the words are emotional, full of guilt, self-pity, and the certitude of ultimate love and rest: and wiry and shrill and lacking in the massiveness it needs, the singing nevertheless achieves the beginnings of its purpose. Nearly everyone gets warmed up and sings louder, the lilt and swing and improvisation become less inhibited, and a kind of ticklish, intensely sexual laughter and triumph begins to work at the mouth and to shine in the eyes.

Only it never quite breaks loose even from the shame that poisons it, and it leaves them shy or masklike or concealing in jokes.

People come in and go out as they like; smoke at the doorway. There is no formal end to the service. The children and men drift out, then the wives: for the last half hour only Tingle and his two girls and Mrs. Tingle (moved, serious, and nearly silent in her deep black) are left in the shack.

It is seldom they have a sermon. A year ago last fall a Nazarene preacher named Mr. Eddie Sellers,

from up above Tuscaloosa, preached them two in successive days, and taught them a new hymn he had written. He really satisfied them, and they still remember him with deep gratitude.

PREVIOUS SPREAD: HOUSE FROM REAR

CHAPTER 9

Health

How late in her pregnancy a woman works around the house and in the fields and how soon she gets back to work again depends on her health and how much grit she has. Since that is the code she believes in and lives up to the answer is, she works as late and soon as she can stand to, which is likely to mean later and sooner than she should.

A granny-woman charges five dollars for delivery, a doctor twenty-five. The Burroughses are flat-footed in their preference for doctors. The Fieldses and Tingles have used both: which, depending on haste, state of mind, and the willingness to take on the debt. (With no phones and town seven miles off, getting a doctor takes a while.) Fields prefers a doctor though: you never can tell when things will go wrong. The Tingles don't much believe in doctors for anything; they prefer woods-cures.

Of the seven children the Tingles have lost, one lived to be four, and pulled a kettle of scalding water over on him. (Such accidents, with milder results, are not infrequent in large families with distracted mothers.) One lived to be five and ate some bad bologna sausage one night and was dead before morning. The rest died within their first year. One died of colitis. From what people said of it another must have died of infantile paralysis. The rest, they don't know what they died of, the doctor never told them. William Fields's twin died winter before last, of pneumonia. Last winter William was very sick, too. He got choking spells and his face got as black as a shoe. The doctor has told them that unless his tonsils are removed he may not live through another winter. They don't know whether or not to believe him; meantime there are other expenses already incurred that they can't afford as it is. The Burroughses' daughter Martha Ann was six months old when she died. The doctor found out what it was but there was nothing he could do about it. It was an abscess behind the eye.

Floyd says, "You ain't never seen trouble till you lose a youngun."

If you bring a child through its first year or two though, its chances are a lot better. Charles had a terrible siege of pneumonia last winter; his skin is still the color of skimmed milk; but he lived through it. He also lived through the chills that came on in the spring, but that was easier. Everyone gets the chills. You know when one is coming on when your back feels like it is going to break. The best thing to break a chill is quinine. Three Sixes is good, too, and if you haven't got the money for quinine or 666 there is bitterweed: make a tea of nine of the yellow flowers and drink it. Elizabeth boiled up twenty-seven of them in a dose and it done her might a good. There are three kinds of chill, the dumb chill, the shaking chill, and the congestive chill. The dumb chill is mildest; that's what you generally get. The shaking chill is much worse. Mary Fields had such a bad one that even when she was held down on the bed the bed rattled on the floor. The congestive chill, Frank Tingle has had. His face got as black as a wool hat and everyone, including the doctor, thought sure he would die. A man only lives through three of them, and he has had two.

Nobody escapes malaria and its returns; and in its milder forms, such as diarrhea, nausea, headache, dizziness, sudden departures of strength, and retching of bile, everyone takes it for granted. Every so often, though, you get such a bad spell of it you mighty nigh have to quit work. Soda and Calotabs are the common remedies. The Tingles like this one, to begin a meal: a pinch of Epsom salts three times a day for nine days; skip nine days; resume; go on until relieved. About a pound generally fixes you up.

Or if you are constituted luckily, the various poisons with which your system is loaded will assemble themselves into the safety valves locally known as risings and more widely known as boils. After a while, the valve blows off. That is the signal for another rising. Ruby, late last summer, was developing one in the fold of the elbow the size of a dollar watch. Her mother had had nine in the past month. Their arms and legs were leopardlike with violet scars. The doctor was quite jolly about it, in a way doctors have. He told them every rising was worth five dollars to them.

Mrs. Tingle prefers the more violent work of the fields, in the hot sun, to housework, because so long as she is sweating and working hard in the sun the rheumatism doesn't clamp into her joints so bad. She has also had pellagra, for the past ten years, and they have spent a great deal, they have no idea how much, trying to get it cured. The hard time she has eating we have spoken of. Three years ago she was out of her head for a long time. That was when Ida Ruth was a baby. Once she tried to kill Ida Ruth with a chunk of stovewood. She is better now and thinks it must be the powders, that is to say, the yeast. For the past year and a half she has been taking Brewer's Yeast stirred up in molasses, milk, and water. She still has nervous spells though and they are bad. She can feel them coming on like something terrifying sneaking up behind her and then all of a sudden she sees black and yellow lights busting all around and after that she doesn't know anything for a while.

Floyd Burroughs has spells, too, of a different kind. He falls down and foams at the mouth just like a dog and it scares Allie Mae and the children something awful. For a while he was having those spells as often as twice a week. He hasn't had them though, since they moved to this new place, and it seems to

Allie Mae like God must have been on their side and told them to move.

Allie Mae has the beginnings of a cataract. Mrs. Tingle, her aunt, has one still further advanced and treats it with camphor water. Mrs. Tingle's mother and one of her aunts went blind with them.

Allie Mae has bad pains in the stomach from time to time, not at all the ordinary indigestion pains, that frighten her badly: her mother and her grandmother both died of cancer.

Her father Bud Fields has a skin cancer, in the right shoulder. On the surface it doesn't look like anything but it has worked down under the collarbone and into the shoulder muscle. He had his choice of have it cut out or treated with X-rays and, in fear for his throat, chose the less tangible treatment. He spent the midsummer in silent and deep terror of death: walked and bummed his way to Moundville and thence was taken to Tuscaloosa for the X-rays; three treatments. The thing that frightened him worst of all was the ether. In extreme nausea you feel like death, and he took that to mean quite literally that he was dying. No one thought to explain, and though he was advised to lie down and get over the effects no one got insistent when, not having warned his wife of any length of absence, he chose rather to get back home as fast as possible. The doctor who had taken him up dropped him still jellified with ether-nausea, at Moundville, to walk the seven miles home.

Presumably they caught the cancer in time. He was strongly advised to do no work for two weeks, then to come back. The cotton was ready though, and he spent the days picking.

They were good to him about this cancer: the charge will be only $50, plus the Moundville doctor's treatments and, likely as not, his transportation.

Both Burroughs and Tingle have appendix trouble. Tingle lay eight solid days under the ice cap; Floyd used it for three days, late last spring. (Mrs. Peoples came down with appendicitis late in the summer and there was another rush call for Tingle's ice cap.) An operation would run you into debt and put you out of work: it's wiser to freeze it and trust to luck.

Excepting Mrs. Tingle, none in the three families show any signs of pellagra: doubtless the butter and green foods are just about sufficient to stave it off.

Whether or not there is hookworm, is hard to say. Charles's anemic pallor may be a symptom of it, but Charles has been very sick. The halting of Squeaky's growth may be a result of it; and on the other hand may be some glandular sprain. (William Fields's abnormal size must be due to the same glandular disequilibrium which produces half the sheriffs you will see in the South.) None of the children were dirt-eaters, outside the normal course of getting down their meals.

Down around Greensboro, the county seat, where nearly all the tenants are Negroes, doctors still charge what they did in the horse-and-buggy days: a dollar a mile, not of course including services and prescriptions. The Moundville doctors have come down on their price; one charges five and the other three for a trip to Mills Hill. Why the five-dollar man can get away with it and why Moundville's third doctor, a young man, has not yet built up much of a practice, is explicable only as many other things in the deep country are: by the power of habit. None of the three families has any clear idea what the state of their health costs them from year to year: we

SADIE TINGLE

can only assume that it is one of the more reliable drains on the pocketbook, though even Burroughs uses doctors very little. Patent medicines are somewhat steadily used. The Fieldses have a little bottle of pills that cover a multitude of evils: green pills for the liver, white for the stomach, morphine for misery. Mrs. Fields is a great believer in the efficacy of asafetida dissolved in whiskey for almost anything from a bad cold on. Mrs. Tingle knows a great deal about home and woods remedies and exchanges knowledge and the roots of herbs with the Negroes: swampwillow bark for chills; queen's delight for pellagra; heart leaves for heart trouble; blacksnake root for chills; cottonseed poultices for head pains; snuff poultices for pneumonia; rattlesnake grease or polecat oil for rheumatism (but best of all for that is alligator grease). She keeps a big assortment of roots and leaves on hand ready for immediate use and turns up with advice and offers all over the neighborhood the minute anybody is sick. Floyd and Allie Mae won't take the teas; Frank Tingle won't allow a doctor across his doorstep; the Fieldses in this matter as in most others are midway.

Invariably people work as long as they can stand up to it, and this is as much out of tradition and pride as of necessity and poverty. It is the same with death. Frank Tingle had seven uncles and every one but one died with his shoes on, and that one had one shoe on and died trying to pull on the other one. Tingle and Fields and Burroughs have all taken out burial insurance and all of them have had to let their policies lapse. People use undertakers now more than they used to; it is almost customary. The undertaker's charge is $25, to take the corpse and bury it. It is seldom that anyone goes in for extras, such as embalming, or a headstone. Women lay out the corpse; everyone sits up with it; women, more especially the older women, wail, and tear their hair at the burial; at either end of the bare clay mound is a driven pine board, sometimes plain, sometimes sawed to the rough shape of an hourglass. Offerings are set in the clay along with ridge of the grave: a horse shoe; or a dead electric bulb; or a pretty piece of glass or china; or a china statuette of a comic bulldog; or a child's tea set; or a Coca Cola bottle; or mussel shells: sometimes a few flowers. When the flowers are done for, that is likely to be the end of it. Ordinarily people do not travel far during their lifetime; but they move, and abandon, often enough so that there is scarcely more feeling for the dead than for the land they have farmed or the homes they have lived in.

APPENDIX I

On Negroes

I n the interests of keeping the subject as clear as possible the main body of this article is devoted to a study of cotton tenancy in terms of white families only. But one tenant in three is a Negro. There is no space here to do him justice, nor shall that be attempted. In lieu of that, here are a few notes, almost at random.

You should know to begin with that there are terms on which Negroes and whites in the South have unselfconscious and even friendly relationships. You should know also how easily the Southern white can flare into murder, offered terms he does not care for. The Negro fits into the structure of cotton tenancy as he fits into the structure of Southern labor: as a man the white laborer is born hating and dies hating. The Negro is hated because he is a nigger; he is hated because it is believed that no unguarded white woman is safe within a mile of him; he is hated because he will work for wages a white man would spit on and will take treatment a white man would kill for; he is worst hated, of course, by whites who by the force of circumstance are anywhere near as low in the social scale as he. Needless perhaps to say, he works for what wages are offered him because he has to live, and he takes what treatment is handed him because any objection could mean death. White tenants who despise him, nevertheless—and they are tenants who have never had the benefit of clarification from organizers—are here and there beginning to conclude that their actual enemy is not the man who accepts lower offers than they will but the man who makes them and forces him to them; and they are able even to realize that should they through any organization attempt to assert themselves, it will be absolutely necessary that the Negroes be in the same organization.

When Southern New Dealers and liberals and indeed anyone critical of the South and interested in improving matters there insist how important it is that the work be done by those who Understand the Ways There they are to a certain extent dead right: an Understanding of the Ways is an almost indispensable advantage, deprived of which you are all but certain to pull incredible bloomers. But since by that understanding they also mean an understanding which will not Make Trouble: since they mean that the Race Problem should be treated sympathetically and a hundred per cent ineffectually: their opinion is only just so good. If the Christian Millennium could be initiated as simply as a President opening a baseball season, all would be well. As it is, the South is involved more deeply and tragically than pure reasonableness and understanding can extricate. No white Southerner is responsible for his ideas of the Negro and his place nor even for the dangerousness of his reflexes against the Negro, since essentially they are actuated by a subconscious but nonetheless mortal fear. And no Negro is responsible for the gigantic weight of physical and spiritual brutality he has borne and is bearing. And it is tragic that irresponsible persons should brain each other. But it seems quite inevitable that that, sooner or later, is what any beginning of a solution will come to.

NEGRO CHILDREN

There are white tenants quite as bad-off as the least-fortunate Negro tenants. There are Negro foremen, Negro overseers, Negro small-farmers, and even Negro landlords. Generally speaking though, the Negro is a lot worse off, on the land, than the white man. Consider the status of the white families written of here. It is not too hot. Then take away the garden. And the hog that is killed for winter meat. And the cow. And reduce the amount of corn and peas and sorghum. And add a general tendency, among landlords, to enjoy cheating a Negro who, used to being cheated, enjoys getting away with everything he can; and make a vicious circle of that. Add also the amused encouragement the landlord gives, in the course of friendly kidding, to bastardy and the breakup of families. Add those tones of whining or clowning servility which most favorably impress most landlords and which most thoroughly destroy personal integrity. Add the often sincere yet always curiously measured kindness of landowners in cancelling a nigger's debt, when it is hopeless enough; in helping him out of jail, when it is only a razor fight or something else more characteristic of a Negro than any assertion of his human rights: for which the reward is anything between a beating and a murder. Keep on adding in one detail after another, and you get a creature so certified for disease, so lacking in possibilities of self-respect, so starved, and so abysmally ignorant, that you can scarcely wonder how few Southern whites are capable of thinking of the Negro as a human being.

Venereal disease is thick among them. Salvarsan was for a while provided by the State at a cost of nineteen cents a shot; now it is back at its customary drugstore price: $1.50 a shot; which is prohibitive to most Negroes and to many whites. Malaria flowers as richly on their blood as on white. The skins of many are rusty with what can be merely ill health, and what can be pellagra. By the thousands they are reduced, in the winter, to a diet precisely short of death by starvation. Since they are thickest in the land first settled, and cleared by their race, firewood is in many places scarce. In the south half of Hale County last winter, the worst in ten years, it was all but nonexistent. They are terribly susceptible to pneumonia. The floors of their houses are low to the ground in the wet cold winter. They are much too ignorant and much too habituated to the idea of work to take to their beds in time. One Negro in Marion, Alabama, who happened not to be an exaggerative type, told of sixteen farm Negroes within his acquaintance who died of pneumonia last winter. Their babies die off like flies in autumn. They use midwives and conjure women for birth and sickness, partly out of mistrust of doctors, partly out of superstition, partly out of poverty. The midwife's charge is five dollars or barter. Sometimes a baby is given as pay. One Hale County midwife objected at length when she got paid the fourth baby in a row from the same mother.

To say that they are carefree is simply asinine. To say that they are distinguished for their joy in living as clearly as whites of the corresponding class are distinguished for slowness and sadness in living is simply true. That they are rich in emotion and grace and almost supernaturally powerful as beings, is hard not to see. They dress in a sense of beauty no other American people approaches; they are creating perhaps the most distinguished American lyric art of their time; the "non-creative" are sympathetic to art and to delicacies of feeling and conduct as the general white people have not been for three centuries; they love with a lewd grace and fall out of love with a frankness that few Western whites can have managed since the time of St. Paul: and in short it is somewhat difficult to believe, in the course of watching a few thousand of them going through the alienated motions of their living, that they are not in several important respects not merely an equal but a superior race: and that what they have gone through during the past few generations has not contributed so much to that superiority as nature ever did, and as much as intelligence ever can.

APPENDIX 2

Landowners

The Southern landowner, the keystone of the social and economic structure of the rural South, is an almost inconceivably subtle and complex problem. We can hope in this limited space only to make a very few general things clear about him which by some odd chance seem not to be clear.

He is not something done up in gum boots, a blacksnake whip, and a gun. He is not something rigged out in a black string tie, quotation from Horace and Stark Young, and a set of Maxwell House julep strainers. He is neither Simon Legree nor Old Cuhnel Chahteris nor is he likely to be whatever is meant by a Southern Gentleman but he is, strange as it may seem, a provincial, bigoted, powerful, and essentially innocent human being who in all his mind and heart and flesh is soaked in believing, beyond any need for conscious or even much unconscious hypocrisy, the things which a human being in his economic and social and historical situation would be bound to believe. There is not room to go into these beliefs, either. It must suffice to say that they justify him, in his eyes, in his position and livelihood and in any conceivable ramification of his relationship with his tenants. Within his structure of belief he has room to be "good" and "honest" or "evil" and "ruthless" or just an indifferent mixture. Generally, like any other member of society as it is today, he is an indifferent mixture. It must never be forgotten that it is neither his vocation nor his joy to cheat or intimidate or squeeze blood from his tenants. He is the owner of more or less land, farmed by tenants and planted to cotton, and it is his business to make as much money as he can. There, as elsewhere, that invariably and inevitably entails the harming of human beings far beyond the poor power of good or evil intention to help much or much further to harm: and there, as elsewhere, it by no means inevitably entails the deliberate misuse of human beings. It is safe to say that the average landlord's relationship with and, even, treatment of his tenants is, on the purely human or consciously

CABIN

moral plane, several degrees more personal and, even more just and friendly, than the relationship between, say, the average manufacturer and his employees.

It is further safe to say that he thinks of his tenants, white or black, neither exactly as he would think of human beings nor exactly as he would think of his mules: he just thinks of them as tenants, and thus treats them, and thus demands that they act and treat themselves. It is also safe to say that he is more fully at ease with Negro than with white tenants and therefore, in a certain sense, likes and even "treats" them better. Here follows some direct and some indirect quotations of an assortment of landowners, ranging from big-time to small-time:

These people, these tenants, get everything they need: land to farm, a house to live in, food to eat and plenty of it, clothes to cover their nakedness. We loan them money for whatever they need it for; we advance them their fertilizer; I want to ask you what they'd do without us. They get schooling, too, and who pays the taxes for that? It's the landowners that pays them. Moreover they don't risk a thing on the crop; it's the land-lord that runs the risk. Yes, they get all they need, and they're contented, all of them but a few sore-heads who think the world owes them a living, and they don't want any better and wouldn't know what to do with it if they had it. They are every one of them ignorant, they are most of them shiftless, and they are nearly all of them improvident. When they get a little money they spend it like water on pretty clothes, or liquor, or on autos if they have enough. There's not one in a hundred of them that had any idea of the value of money, or any idea of saving. There's not one in any hundred who could run his own farm, un-supervised, into anything but ruin. There is not one in twenty who would want to try. Of course there are landlords who take an unfair advantage of their tenants, just as there are dishonest busi-nessmen in any business: and so, too, there are tenants who are in a bad way. You can in fact find just whatever you are looking for. But what these Northerners write about it is just a big pack of downright lies, that's all. Anyone that stays in the South long enough to learn the ways sees how it is.

All this talk about mistreatment of tenants. Sure, maybe they is some of it here and there, they's sons of bitches in ever walk of life. But I can tell you if you lined up a hundred of them in a row that was bad off and sure enough found out about them you'd find ninety-nine of them was bad off through nobody's fault but their own, because they was ignorant, and because they was shifluss. Their people was tenants before them, and *their* people was tenants before *that*.

We give 'em the free land for a meeting house. Keeps 'm out of a devilment.

I got a great admiration for that nigger. I tell you, if that man wasn't a nigger he'd a gone a long ways in the world.

Niggers make better tenants than white men do. They're more contented and less likely to get independent. They stay on one place longer, generally. Lots of them stays with you all their lives, and their father before them and their young ones after.

They don't have nothn to worry about; no responsibility; nothn to lose. Ever thang's furnished them. All they got to do is work and six months a the year they don't even have to do that. (This was said of whites as well as of Negroes.)

All my tenants are niggers. Always have been, always will be. I'll tell you the honest fact. I'm *afraid* of white tenants; scared some of them would up and kill me one day. (Two other landlords agreed with the first on this.)

We get along all right with our niggers around here and we don't have to say or do nothn neither. They know what would happen if they started anything.

Why I'm mighty fond of my niggers. I get along beautifully with my niggers. Why I never hit a nigger in my life.

You hear all this talk of bad treatment. Now I ask you: would a good farmer mistreat his mules?

Those nigger burial societies are a mighty good thing. Why I had one die on me last week and it didn't cost me a penny.

I tell you you got to go to outfigure a nigger.

We do all we can for them and then they will prodyuce a little more.

They git all that's coming to them and more.

The essential structure of the South is, of course, economic: cold and inevitable as the laws of chemistry. But that is not how the machine is run. The machine is run on intuition, and the structures of intuition are delicate and subtle as they can be only in a society which is not merely one thing but two: a dizzy mixture of feudalism and of capitalism in its latter stages. Moreover, everyone born in the South, and no one born outside it, has a nose for this intensely specialized chemistry of local intuition: so that relationships between landlord and tenants are settled and crystallized, as a rule, quietly and even inarticulately. A tenant knows to a hair's breadth just when and where he is out of line and just how to get back on it. Usually he does get back on it, and there is no further "trouble." If he doesn't, there is the whole natural system of boycott mentioned in the article. And if these things fail there is, quite naturally, violence.

Because so much goes by intuition and the power of custom, and because the trap the tenant is caught in is not only as huge as the structure of his civilization but as intimate as every breath he draws, the

PREVIOUS SPREAD: COTTON AND CORN

general inter-class tone or taste of air in the South is peculiarly tranquil. It is a tranquility both real and deceptive. It is real, and importantly real, simply because it exists. It is deceptive because of what it takes the place of, and hides.

It takes the place of, and hides, and is essentially more terrible than, a "terrorism" which becomes necessary only when the enormous, all but hypnotic strength of the tranquility has failed to suffice. The "terrorism" becomes necessary not through moustache-twirling and fiendish deliberation but once again very simply and inevitably and chemically, by intuition and by reflex. It is perfectly irrelevant to law and it goes as far as either as it "needs" or "happens" to. A given landlord may or may not take active physical part in it but you may be sure he countenances it: you may be sure there is not one in any hundred who would think twice about countenancing or, for that matter, instigating it. There is in Southern white man, distributed almost as thickly as the dialect, an epidemic capability of sadism which you would have to go as far to match and whose chief basis is possibly, but only possibly, and only one among many, a fear of the Negro, deeper and more terrible than any brief accounting can suggest or explain. This flaw of sadism can turn its victims loose into extremities which the gaudiest reports have only begun to suggest.

Trouble begins in the galled spots. That, too, is where organizers come; and, later, the sympathizers, the investigators, the reporters. By the time the latter get there all hell has broken loose and there is nothing pretty about it. Through ignorance and shock and rage fully as much as through bias, the reporters take what they find as representative of the South as a whole.

What they find is, to be sure, not a circumstance on what in the course of time seems likely to happen in the South as a whole. But what they find is also not true of the general South as the South is today, and day by day. And if the truth is not only more interesting and more complex but also more valuable than falsehood, then the truth had better be recognized.